Writing Put to the Test:

Teaching for the High-Stakes Essay

Amy Benjamin

EYE ON EDUCATION
6 DEPOT WAY WEST, SUITE 106
LARCHMONT, NY 10538
(914) 833–0551
(914) 833–0761 fax
www.eyeoneducation.com

Library of Congress Cataloging-in-Publication Data

Benjamin, Amy, 1951-
Writing put to the test : teaching for the high stakes essay / Amy
Benjamin.
    p. cm.
  ISBN 1-59667-026-6
  1. English language—Composition and exercises—Study and teaching
(Secondary) I. Title.

LB1631.L387 2006
808.042'0712—dc22

                                                           2006008103

10 9 8 7 6 5 4 3 2 1

Editorial and production services provided by
Richard H. Adin Freelance Editorial Services
52 Oakwood Blvd., Poughkeepsie, NY 12603-4112
(845-471-3566)

Also Available from Eye On Education

Active Literacy Across the Curriculum:
Strategies for Reading, Writing, Speaking, and Listening
Heidi Hayes Jacobs

Writing in the Content Areas, 2nd Edition
Amy Benjamin

Differentiated Instruction:
A Guide for Middle and High School Teachers
Amy Benjamin

Differentiated Instruction:
A Guide for Elementary Teachers
Amy Benjamin

Socratic Seminars and Literature Circles
for Middle and High School English
Victor and Marc Moeller

What Great Teachers Do *Differently:*
14 Things that Matter Most
Todd Whitaker

Seven Simple Secrets:
What the Best Teachers Know and Do
Annette Breaux and Todd Whitaker

Classroom Motivation From A to Z:
How to Engage Your Students in Learning
Barbara Blackburn

Handbook on Differentiated Instruction
for Middle and High Schools
Sheryn Spencer Northey

Reading, Writing and Gender:
Instructional Strategies and Activities
That Work for Girls and Boys
Gail Goldberg and Barbara Roswell

About the Author

Amy Benjamin, a veteran English teacher, trains educators throughout the country in writing across the curriculum, strategic literacy, and differentiated instruction. She has received awards for excellence in teaching from the New York State English Council, Tufts University, and Union College. As president of the Assembly for the Teaching of English Grammar, an affiliate of the National Council of Teachers of English, she is a leading authority on effective ways for teaching both academic and creative writing.

Table of Contents

1

Introducing On-Demand Writing

The purpose of this book is to help educators like you improve your students' ability to write clear, coherent essays in response to on-demand writing prompts. I hope to help you increase your students' scores on VITs (Very Important Tests) without sacrificing sound pedagogy that leads to durable learning.

In this age of high-stakes testing, schools and school districts are compared to each other on the basis of scores on state-mandated tests. Schools that fall short of "adequate yearly progress" (AYP) are exposed and even denounced as "failing schools." The SAT now requires an on-site essay in which students must defend a position in a well-organized, albeit short, essay. Learning to write through a process approach held sway in the 1980s, but writing on demand is what is now expected.

Whether writing on demand yields the best product, the most reflective thinking, or the finest use of language is irrelevant. Obviously, a better piece of writing is going to be produced if the writer has more time to spend on all of the stages of the writing process. Equally obvious is the fact that we write best when we care about the message. Writing on demand to an external prompt is not the natural way to communicate. However, taken for what it is, we need to make our students better at this particular skill.

On-demand writing is unlike the kind of writing that most of us *like* to teach: on-demand writing isn't about creativity, nor is it about self-discovery. It isn't about coaxing and sculpting prose that is a thing of beauty out of the lump of clay that is a rough draft. It isn't about revision. It isn't about editing. *On-demand writing is about the writer's ability to think and write quickly, and to execute the task within a time frame of 20 minutes, a half hour, or 45 minutes at most.*

This is not to say that we should abandon teaching writing through process. Nor is it to say that we should have students write *only* to external prompts, rushing the process to complete the writing task within a time limit. On the contrary, students need to do plenty of writing of all kinds, for various purposes and genres, learning how to adjust language tone to address the expectations of various audiences.

This book will explain why and how we need to extend our writing process instruction so as to prepare students for the high-stakes essay.

1. **Background:** Where are we? How did we get here? Where are we going? Where are we today in terms of writing instruction and society's expectations about what an educated person should be able to do? What are the trends in education that affect writing instruction? Within the profession, how is on-demand writing received? What supports are available? What oppositions confront us as we seek to improve student performance in the on-demand task?

2. **Teaching through rhetorical modes:** When we write to a prompt, we need to orient our minds to the particular type of language (rhetorical mode) that we are being asked to produce. Narrative-descriptive writing is substantially different from persuasive writing in terms of organization, syntax, and diction. Information-based writing, such as reports and explanations, has its own features. So the first task is for the writer to establish a firm grounding in the proper rhetorical environment.

3. **Planning and organization:** When time is of the essence, planning is a key skill. How do we help our students use the allotted time strategically?

4. **Scoring:** Scoring on most high-stakes tests is done by rubric. This part of the book explains the five key traits, what scorers are looking for, and how to instruct for each.

5. **Assistive intervention:** What are the most effective, efficient ways to assist struggling writers, including our English language learners? What do our strong writers know that our weak writers don't know? Where do our weak writers need help the most? Included in this part of the book is a system that I call RxWrite. RxWrite is a collection of prescriptive lessons corresponding to key writing traits. Through RxWrite, you can direct your students to lessons and guided practice pinpointed to their demonstrated needs.

An Analogy:
Rehearsal, Dress Rehearsal, Performance

Musicians and athletes perform on demand, but the quality of their performance is shaped by deliberate practice in the key components. Everyone expects a musician to tune up and warm up, to practice scales for speed and accuracy, and to approach new pieces with deliberation, replaying the tricky parts over and over. And then there's the dress rehearsal, where the musician simulates concert conditions just to get the feel of running through the piece without interruption. Translated into the writing experience, the analogy would look like this:

Figure 1.1. Musician vs. Writer

Student Musician	*Student Writer*
Tune-up, warm-up: The musician establishes a special psychological space for music.	**Conversation:** The student begins to focus on the subject of the writing task by informally gathering ideas together and considering the issues: What do I know? Why do I care? What might I say?
Practicing scales and etudes: The musician builds and maintains the physical agility and mental acuity necessary to create music.	**Prewriting experience:** The student further develops ideas and builds knowledge through reading and continued discussion.
Sight-reading; analyzing the musical text: The musician interprets the symbolic language of musical text, recognizing its patterns, identifying tricky passages, and mentally translating the symbols into sounds.	**Planning and organizing:** The student considers the nature of the prompt and lays out an organizational plan which may include a word inventory, sketch or outline, and tentative thesis.
Rehearsal: Through "informed repetition," the musician prepares the piece, concentrating on the hardest parts. The musician is assisted by an expert coach who gives feedback, modeling, and advice.	**Composing (drafting, revising, and editing):** Over a period of time, the student uses the recursive writing process to create a meaningful, coherent piece of writing.
Dress rehearsal: To instill confidence, the musician simulates concert conditions, pretending that an audience is present. Ideally, the musician is in the actual concert hall, under concert sound and lighting conditions.	**In-class on-demand task:** Given a task similar to that of the standardized test, and given simulated test conditions, the student responds to a writing prompt.
Performance.	**On-demand writing task on a standardized test.**

There are musicians who play for their own enjoyment or for the social experience of making music with others. They are not performers. And there are writers who write for their own clarification or expression. They are not published writers, and may or may not save what they write or have others read it. The practice that they get will make them more fluent. They are developing the level of performance that we call *automaticity:* the ability to function in a complex task without thinking about its discrete steps. It's important for writers to function automatically on the high-stakes essay, and getting to that level requires regular practice. However, practice is not enough: the writer needs instruction, feedback, and expectations that the instruction and feedback will be applied toward a better product. At this point we should look at the tools of modern writing instruction.

Key Terms in Writing Instruction

When I was in high school back in the 1960s, most of the following pedagogical terms regarding writing instruction weren't used among educators. In fact, if writing instruction was done at all, very little of it was thrown my way. I was given assignments, not instruction. Since the Bay Area Writing Project and the National Writing Project revolutionized the teaching of English language arts in the 1970s, educators have developed a lexicon to talk about the writing process. And since No Child Left Behind (NCLB) legislation, that lexicon has grown to include language about the high-stakes essay test.

Anchor Papers

Anchor papers are papers that the test-makers provide to show what they expect scores at different levels of the scoring range to look like. The test-makers comment on the anchor papers, explaining how they arrived at the grade. Evaluators are expected to read the anchor papers and their commentary carefully to come to agreement about how they are to judge the papers. This process must be done as a group immediately before individuals assign value to the papers. The examination and discussion of anchor papers is time-consuming, but it is absolutely necessary to maintain the integrity of the grades.

Diction

Diction is word choice. In academic writing, we expect the writer to use subject-area language that is as elevated, specific, and technical as possible. Most students need to learn academic diction through explicit instruction.

Document-Based Question

Going by the abbreviation DBQ, the document-based question is widely used in social studies classes. The experience of writing to answer a document-based question is that of an on-the-spot compression of a research paper, except that the sources are presented right there for the writer to use. Given several primary source documents—for example, political cartoons, advertisements, newspaper articles, public notices, or personal correspondence—the writer must put together an essay in response to a prompt. The writer is required to use the documents as supportive evidence.

Expository Writing

Often used in contrast to creative writing, expository writing exposes (explains, describes, justifies) a subject. The term itself, once a staple in English classes, is not used much anymore, but those who still use it do so with the expectation that everyone knows what they mean.

Five-Paragraph Essay

The five-paragraph essay is a convenient structure for on-demand writing. This structure, once a staple in schoolroom writing, now languishes in disrepute as a hackneyed form suitable for only the most perfunctory, desultory writing. There's nothing inherently good or bad about the five-paragraph essay, except that weaker writers probably benefit by learning it as a structure, whereas stronger ones may find it limiting.

Formulaic Writing

The five-paragraph essay is an example of formulaic writing. By formulaic writing, we mean writing that fits into a recognizable standard structure. The writer places certain kinds of information in certain slots of a discursive structure. Some formulas are so rigid that they assign a number to every sentence. Although many people criticize formulaic writing for being uncreative, most experienced teachers find that formulas are very helpful for struggling writers. Critics of formulaic writing disdain it as "inauthentic"; however, most genres adhere to a formula, or at least follow a standard form.

Group Scoring

For many state-mandated tests, teachers are required to score as a group. The group receives detailed instructions, rubrics, and sample (anchor) papers representing various degrees of quality. Through a well-organized procedure, the group reads the anchor papers carefully to align their judgments with what the test-makers expect. Often, more than one reader is required to read each paper independently, not knowing the score given by the other reader. In cases where there is a significant discrepancy, a third reader (also blind) is given the paper.

Harvard Outline

A Harvard outline is the classic outline form that shows a hierarchical structure between main ideas and supportive details. The Harvard outline lays ideas out through a system of indentation, where subordinating ideas are indented progressively. Every level of the hierarchy must have at least two facts. No complete sentences are to be used in a Harvard outline. Tiers in the Harvard outline are designated by alternating Roman numerals with letters, with descending tiers signified by lower case letters.

Holistic Scoring

In holistic scoring, the evaluator gives the writing piece a once-over and makes a quick judgment based upon its effectiveness as a whole. Scorers of high-stakes essays, although they read the papers quickly, are supposed to hone and standardize their judgments in accordance with rubrics and anchor papers.

National Writing Project (NWP)

The National Writing Project, born in Berkeley, California, along with the landmark Bay Area Writing Project, is a venerated institution that has outposts at universities around the United States.

On-Demand Writing

What we mean by on-demand writing is that the writer is given a prompt and asked to execute a response to the prompt in a specified amount of time. The writer needs to compress the writing process to include prewriting, planning, and drafting. Very little time remains available to the writer for revision or editing. The chief reason for on-demand writing is summative assessment.

Paraphrasing

Paraphrasing is the process of extracting main ideas and details but putting them in the writer's own words. To do this the writer needs to change both the sentence structure and the key vocabulary. Some teachers go by the "four-word rule," which states that the paraphrase cannot contain more than four words in a row that are identical to the original. Paraphrasing differs from summary, which condenses the information into main ideas. Paraphrasing is a rewording that also involves combining individual sentences.

Peer Editing

Peer editing is a process wherein students exchange papers and become each other's critics and proofreaders. Many teachers supply checklists to focus the readers on specific traits.

Prompt

The word "prompt" has popularly taken the place of "question" or "topic" to indicate what the content and length of a piece of writing is to be.

Reader-Based Writing

Reader-based writing is writing with the reader's needs and expectations *foremost* in mind. The reader-based writer, mindful of what the reader's attitude and prior knowledge are going to be, consciously facilitates the reader's job. Reader-based writing involves a lot of signals and guideposts within the text so that the reader can navigate through it easily. In reader-based writing, the writer is not engaging in the digressive self-discovery process that writing often becomes when it drifts toward what the writer wants to express rather than what the reader wants to read.

Rhetoric

Rhetoric is specialized, deliberate language with the purpose of having a specific effect.

Rhetorical Modes

Rhetorical language organizes itself into several patterns, each characterized by its own tendencies. The three major rhetorical modes are narrative, informative, and persuasive. But these modes can be broken down further into description, cause and effect, classification, comparison/contrast, definition, example, and process analysis. These categories are variable, and writing teachers have different ways of naming them.

Rubric

A rubric is a scoring guide that lays out, trait by trait, how a writing piece is evaluated. Rubrics are usually presented as tables, with the rows naming the writing traits and the columns indicating the point value along a continuum of how well the writer achieved success for each trait (see *Traits* in the following text).

Scaffolding

Scaffolds facilitate the execution of a task by providing some of the steps, already completed. Suppose a student couldn't organize and develop a writing task. The teacher could provide a completed outline from which the student could go the rest of the way. After some practice, the student might need only a partial outline, then just the bare bones of an outline, and finally be able to conjure an outline independently.

Syntax

Syntax is sentence structure. When we speak of a writer's use of syntax, we are speaking both functionally and stylistically. Functionally, the sentences need to be constructed in a clean, clear manner to support the message unimpeded. Stylistically, the syntax should employ those rhetorical elements, such as parallel structure and repetition, that will imbue the language with grace and elegance.

Traits

Most rubrics recognize the following key traits of writing:

- *Addressing the task.* The extent to which the writer interprets the question and delivers the answer in the expected way.

- *Development.* The extent to which the writer provides main and subordinate ideas.

- *Organization.* The extent to which the writer pursues a form that facilitates comprehension.

- *Language.* The extent to which the writer uses diction and syntax that is interesting and appropriate.

- *Conventions and presentation.* The extent to which the writer has observed the rules of standard written English; the extent to which the writing is legible and the paper inviting to the reader.

Visual Organizer

Also called a graphic organizer or a mind map, a visual organizer is a writing plan laid out on paper that helps the writer establish a relationship between main ideas and supportive details. Writers use visual organizers as a prewriting strategy that will form the structure of the essay. Visual organizers help writers to think in patterns.

Because rhetorical modes also form patterns, each rhetorical mode has a visual organizer to which it is best suited.

Voice, Style, Tone

I've grouped these terms because they are often used interchangeably. Voice, style, and tone refer to the writer's overall attitude toward both the subject and the reader. This attitude is expressed through diction (word choice) and syntax (sentence structure). *Voice* is the writer's personality coming through. Voice is expressed through *style,* the writer's tendency to use certain kinds of grammatical structures. Voice and style combine to produce *tone,* which reveals whether the writer is playful or serious, formal or informal, sympathetic or angry, pleased or resentful, and so on.

Writing Process

The writing process is conceived as a series of stages that bring forth a product worthy of being read by others. The first stage, prewriting, consists of two parts. The first of these is marshaling the necessary information, often through conversation. Then, the would-be writer brainstorms, opening his or her mind to a flurry of uncensored ideas. The writer then transitions into the second stage, composition, by using some form of a visual organizer or listing technique to nail some key ideas in place. The composition stage can be spontaneous or disciplined, depending on the requirements of the task. The next stage is revision, and in processed writing some time should elapse between the stages of composition and revision to allow for objectivity and to give time for more ideas to generate. In the revision stage, the writer becomes more reader-based, more aware of the need for form. Some changes that the writer can be directed to make during the revision stage include eliminating redundancy, providing transitions, enriching the language, and strengthening key points. Many teachers turn the classroom into a community of writers at this point, allowing for feedback from other readers, and many teachers supply reader–writer response questions inviting positive and negative feedback. It is at the next stage, editing, that the writer corrects surface errors. Finally, the piece is "published" in one form or another, and the writer's ideas are presented for their intended purpose: communication.

With this as your introduction, you are in a position to understand what you can do to improve student performance on the high-stakes essay test. What you read in Part I will ground you in the evolution of writing instruction to help you understand the kind of education that your students have probably received heretofore.

I

The High-Stakes Essay

2

Writing Instruction in the Age of Testing

When it comes to public perceptions of student achievement, people consider the ability to write clearly, coherently, and correctly a high priority. In 2003 the National Commission on Writing in America's Schools and Colleges issued a report titled, "The Neglected R: The Need for a Writing Revolution." This report, commissioned by the College Board (the entity responsible for the SAT exams), posits that writing should be a central element in every classroom and challenges American schools to make it so:

> American education will never realize its potential as an engine of opportunity and economic growth until a writing revolution puts writing and communication in their proper place in the classroom. Writing is how students connect the dots in their knowledge. Although many models of effective ways to teach exist, both the teaching and practice of writing are increasingly shortchanged throughout the school and college years. (p. 6)

The report recommends that the amount of writing that schools require should be at least doubled, and that writing be assessed in addition to short answer–type tests as part of state assessment.

No wonder, then, that as of 2005 the SAT instituted an essay component as well as a grammar component. (The alternative to the SAT, the ACT, does not have a mandatory writing component, but it does have a section that calls for choosing the sentence in a group that adheres most closely to standard written English.) On the SAT, the student must compose a coherent essay that takes a position on a given statement, and the student must do so within a time limit. The grammar component of the SAT, like the ACT, tests the student's ear for correctness and efficiency in sentence structure and textual cohesion. Because every school wants its students to achieve well on the SAT, writing skills are high on the agenda for all stakeholders.

But even if the SAT were not our concern, we would still have to attend sharply to writing instruction because all states now require that students demonstrate writing proficiency on their high-stakes tests, at least on the English language arts assessments. And many states do require writing for other subject areas, notably social studies and science. In New York state, students write in response to document-based questions for the fifth-grade state assessments. A student's ability to demonstrate knowledge through writing sends a powerful message. That demonstration of knowledge, in turn, sends a powerful message to the community that translates into the reputation of the school district.

Administrators who are responsible for staff development are keenly aware of the need to build capacity in teachers to make them better teachers of writing. The key questions are these:

- How do we transition students from employing the writing process, in which students craft a piece of writing over time and with assistance, to writing the timed essay, in which they must execute a writing task against the pressure of a time limit and with no outside assistance? How do we achieve a balance so that students are able to use what they've learned through process pedagogy to write on demand and within a time limit?

- How do we offer students sufficient in-class practice for the timed essay without sacrificing precious instructional time?

- What do students need to learn about grammar and mechanics, and how do we integrate such instruction with the other elements of writing, such as organization and development?

- How do we build capacity in all teachers, not just those who teach English language arts, so that they bring more writing into their curricula?

- What formative assessments will effectively translate into higher scores on our writing assessments?

How has writing instruction changed over the past several generations? Since World War II, attitudes about what kind of writing needs to be done in schools and how writing should be taught have undergone four transformations. I'll call these the Age of Product, the Age of Process, the Age of Voice, and now, the Age of Testing. We should view these phases not as discrete demarcations, in which we scoff at previous views about how writing should be taught and what kind of writing should be done. Rather, we should look on each as paving the way for the next, as society changes because of technology, immigration patterns, democratization, and an overall enlightenment about educational opportunities and the people who should have them.

I'll talk about the current landscape first, and then swing back to the phases that brought us here. In writing this book, I've accepted the reality and acceded to the demands of that harsh taskmaster, the standardized test. I've read the objections and lamentations of those who decry the standardized test with its high-stakes essay, considering it antithetical to good writing process instruction. Says the National Council of Teachers of English (NCTE): "The SAT and ACT timed writing tests are "unlikely to improve writing instruction," and have the potential to "compromise student writers and undermine longstanding efforts to improve writing instruction in the nation's schools." The educational leaders who make up the NCTE disapprove of the high-stakes timed essay because they suspect that it will result in a widening gap between economic classes. They suspect that the SAT essay, like its short answers, will be "coachable," thus privileging those who can afford private test-preparation courses and coaches even more. And they lament that teachers will devote undue time to preparing students for this particular type of writing, time that they feel would be better spent teaching students to develop their own "voices" in a variety of genres.

Opponents of the high-stakes timed essay are right about one thing: the test-makers have our attention. But although that is true, I would like us to view the demands on us as an opportunity to improve education. I'm hoping that we can embrace the challenge not by limiting writing instruction to test-prep short-term teaching, but by expanding the repertoire of techniques and experiences that we offer to make students better writers and thinkers.

From the Age of Product to the Age of Process

What brings us to this point in writing instruction? When we look at writing pedagogy since World War II, we find a tectonic shift taking place somewhere in the late 1970s. This is the shift into the pedagogy known as *writing process*. Writers have always engaged in a recursive process in which they brew ideas, tack them down in a recognizable form, and then craft them into something worthy of a reader. But writing was not commonly *taught* as a process. Rather, writing was usually not taught, but *assigned*. Until the "writing process revolution," what passed for writing instruction were activities such as the following:

- Exercises in a grammar book intended to teach the writer how to avoid mechanical errors
- Instruction in outlining, usually using the traditional Harvard outline
- Experiences in writing for various rhetorical modes
- Answering questions with complete sentences

It was at an event known as the Dartmouth Conference in 1966 that the idea of teaching writing as a process was hatched. The now-famous writing process takes the writer back and forth through the following steps:

- *Prewriting experience.* This is time set aside for the writer to come up with freestyle ideas. Rich language experiences such as brainstorming, reading, conversation, and picture-making are encouraged as a way for the writer to open up the floodgates of ideas.

- *Drafting.* In the drafting phrase, the writer captures some of the best ideas that have been set in motion by beginning to form them into a composition. The drafting may feel spontaneous to the writer. The piece may take off on its own, as might a memoir or a personal letter. In the writer's mind, the audience may be the self. The drafting phase may feel heady, set aloft by the freedom of expression that the writer is encouraged to have.

- *Revision and communication.* At this point, the classroom is supposed to turn into a writer's workshop, with our young, exuberant writers sharing their works-in-progress and becoming one another's "critical friends." As critical friends they ask for elaboration and clarification. The process works best when everyone in the workshop is *not* producing the same thing. This individuation happens when writers are writing personal narratives, poems, and other self-sponsored topics.

- *Editing.* It is only at this stage that writers "clean up" their mechanical lapses, and again may do so with a little help from their friends.

- *Publication.* Because writers produce their best work when they care about communication, the writing experience should culminate in a reading experience for someone. The pieces may be posted in the classroom, read aloud, kept in a journal or portfolio, or published in a classroom or schoolwide collection.

That is what writing process instruction looks like, and it works. It works to produce what it is capable of producing: self-sponsored writing pieces that are created for the authentic purpose of communication. It works to get fledgling writers to behave toward writing the way professionals behave: generating ideas, surprising themselves with ideas that spring up, taming those ideas into a recognizable and acceptable form, and conferring with others to generate more ideas and to make sure that our way of communicating is clear. The writing process works best in English language arts classes where students have an open-ended prompt.

So pervasive has writing process instruction been that few teachers have been in the profession long enough to recall what life was like under any other pedagogy. Prior to the writing process approach, writing (if taught at all) was taught in accordance with 19th-century practices that concentrated on writing for the main rhetorical modes. We can arrange writing into a taxonomy that has eight categories: description, narration, cause and effect, classification, definition, exemplification, comparison/contrast, and process analysis. We call these eight categories "rhetorical modes." If you prefer fewer categories, you may combine and reduce the eight modes into three: narration, persuasion, and information. Other taxonomies, such as the one devised by James Kinneavy, speak of writing for four *purposes:* persuasive, expressive, referential, and literary discourse. The important point is that writing instruction followed along the lines of some kind of taxonomy, in which students learned to write in discrete, proscriptive ways.

Taxonomists concerned themselves not with process but with product. The *process* that the writer goes through was considered his or her own business: what counted was the product. We can name this preprocess approach to writing instruction just that: product-based, rather than process-based. Today, the high-stakes timed essay in which the student is given a prompt and expected to write within the limits of academic-sounding language brings us back to product-based writing, to be sure. But perhaps we needn't, to use a favorite cliché of educators, throw the baby out with the bathwater. Perhaps we can improve our product-based instruction by infusing it with what we've learned and come to value in process-based teaching.

Process-based teaching of writing leans toward creative writing, a joy for English teachers. The narrative and descriptive modes of writing are particularly well-suited to the writing process, with its focus on fluency and exploration. If as a result of the Age of Process, the other modes of writing became neglected, WAC (Writing Across the Curriculum, also known as Writing in the Content Areas) enjoyed its own heyday in the 1980s. Just as WAC teachers learned to incorporate process, I believe that we of the High-Stakes Timed Essay Age can incorporate process, albeit a compressed process, as well.

To speak about the writing process is to use the word "nonlinear." By that, we mean that the process is recursive, going back and forth from one step to another. But writing "on demand and on the clock" is linear. Unlike the process-oriented writer, who is finding ideas through the very process of writing them down, the product-oriented writer, operating within a time limit, interprets the question, finds a suitable form, and gets right down to it with barely enough time to reread. A linear process, indeed, and one for which the process-oriented writer may be unprepared without explicit practice in the craft of "getting it down on paper...and fast."

There is no question that teachers of teachers who are best known to promote process-oriented writing (Peter Elbow, Lucy Calkins, and Don Steward, to name a few) favor writing for personal expression. There is no question that we write best about what we care and know the most about. And there is no question that the high-stakes timed essay makes a different kind of demand.

But if we are to truly understand what writing is all about, we need to consider the relationship between process and product. Writing itself is both exploratory and communicative: the writer creates and finds knowledge in the act of writing *and then* figures out a way to communicate such knowledge. It helps immeasurably for the writer to consider the reader's needs and expectations when communicating. Writing, therefore, is a blend between process (exploratory) and product (communicative) orientations. There's the rub: if writing is the means by which we find out what we think, as George Bernard Shaw said of his own writing, then how can anyone be expected to produce a coherent piece on the spot? Does on-demand writing have an internal contradiction that would in fact inhibit—rather than give evidence to—thought?

It is at this point that we need to step back and remember audience and purpose. The audience has needs, and the writer has a purpose. In the case of the high-stakes timed essay, the audience's needs are to find out the following:

- ◆ Can this writer interpret a question?

- ◆ Can this writer develop an idea with generalities and specifics?

- ◆ Can this writer arrange those ideas into the expected form?

- ◆ Is this writer fluent in standard written English, with some stylistic embellishments?

And the writer's purpose, quite simply, is to meet the audience's needs. Under testing conditions, the writer is not looking to find great truths in the universe. Sorry to say, this would not be the time to soul search, to meander, to look under rocks for lurking, undiscovered countries of thought.

Balancing the Trends in Writing Instruction: The Age of Voice

I'd like to get back now to the trends that have informed the teaching of writing even after the process approach established itself. It stands to reason that as the personal narrative became the favored genre in writing classrooms, students' "own voices" grew increasingly welcome. The demands and strictures of standard written English with its pesky conventions began to be seen as unnecessary devices that inhibited free expression. In the early 1980s, the NCTE published and promoted their famous position statement "Students' Right to Their Own Language" (p. 1). English teachers everywhere were encouraged to back off from imposing their own language prejudices upon students, lest they insult the home language and thus fail to nurture the student's natural voice, a voice thought to be authentic and exuberant. The position statement recommended "that NCTE promote classroom practices to expose students to the variety of dialects that comprise our multiregional, multiethnic, and multicultural society, so that they too will understand the nature of American English and come to respect all its dialects." The NCTE asserted that all students, in addition to having a right to read, write, and speak in their home dialect, also have a right to learn the conventions of standard English (which they refer to as "what has been called written edited American English"). This disclaimer notwithstanding, you can see how the river bends away from strict adherence to academic writing of the kind now required.

In the 1980s a movement took wing to employ the English language arts as the vehicle of choice for enacting social change. This social change would manifest itself by eschewing the stranglehold of "written edited American English" in favor of the students' "own language." Patricia Bizzell (1982) spoke of the biases of academia, biases serving to preserve the privileged class by using its dialect while marginalizing other "voices." As English teachers expanded the reading canon to include multicultural voices, writing instruction followed. Insistence on standard English conventions became secondary to reproducing the beauty and cadence of a character's voice.

It should come as no surprise that teachers who bought into the Age of Voice pedagogy were at odds with content-area teachers who wanted students to come to their classes prepared to write coherent answers to content-area questions. And it should come as no surprise that content-area teachers did not view it as *their* job to teach writing. Thus, the tensions between English teachers and content-area teachers tightened, with "the public" weighing in on the side of the content-area teachers. In terms of how education institutions are judged, most people would rather have a workforce of people who know how to write a coherent, clear message in standard English than people who can't do that, but can create character and dialogue.

Into this mix comes e-communication. You might think that educators and parents would cheer upon seeing children and teenagers writing messages to each other on their computers. After all, prior to the e-mail revolution, the personal letter was practically dead as a genre. However, the nature of e-communication is as informal as speech. In fact, e-communication, especially instant messaging (IM), is more like speech than like writing. IMers have blazed a new trail in human communication, one with the back-and-forth nature of dialogue and the symbolism of speech. Although e-communication is the way that people already communicate informally in the workplace, people in admissions offices and human resource departments want to be sure that formal academic writing skills are intact, ready to be called upon when needed.

These conflicting attitudes between the burgeoning informal e-communication styles and the formal academic voice (thought to be an endangered species) plays out in our current Age of Testing. No one is being tested on the ability to write an IM conversation. It wouldn't be much of a leap to attribute the Age of Testing to a backlash against the Age of Voice. Between multicultural education, which many people outside of education resent and mistrust, and the informalities of e-communication, a trend whose lack of adherence to convention would be likely to make people sniff about the end of civilization as we know it, the winds that swept through the 1990s brought about the perfect storm for the Age of Testing.

And Where We Are Now: The Age of Testing

It's naïve and inaccurate to believe that all you have to do to prepare students to write the high-stakes timed essay is teach them to compress the writing process. What is called for is a combination of product- and process-based writing, not the elimination of the former and the time-lapse version of the latter. If you are an administrator responsible for curriculum and instruction, it is important to understand why some of your teachers may not be on board with adapting instruction for the on-demand writing task. The teachers you supervise may be reluctant to leave out steps of the writing process so that students get used to writing within a time limit. They may be reluctant to move away from personal narrative and student-selected topics in favor of prompts.

Teachers need to understand that, like rehearsal and performance, writing process instruction (more like rehearsal) is necessary to build the skills necessary to produce on-demand writing (more like performance).

Summary

The four ages of writing instruction are summarized in Figure 2.1.

Figure 2.1. The Four Ages of Writing Instruction

	The Age of Product	The Age of Process	The Age of Voice	The Age of Testing
Teachers concentrate on	Having students write in various rhetorical modes (categories).	Having students discover their ideas through writing.	Having students develop respect for dialect and language variation.	Having students respond to writing prompts within a time limit.
Teachers believe that	Writing is about fulfilling expectations for various kinds of genres.	Writing is a recursive process that is best when the student chooses the topic and writes for an authentic purpose and real audience.	Writing is a way of expressing authentic human experience, respecting diversity.	They need to simulate test conditions and substance.
Kinds of writing	◆ Argumentation ◆ Comparison/contrast ◆ Answers to specific questions	◆ Personal narratives ◆ Stories, poems, plays	◆ Memoirs ◆ Stories, poems, plays	◆ Informative ◆ Narrative ◆ Persuasive
What is rewarded	◆ Strong organization ◆ Formal, academic language	◆ Personal voice ◆ Humor and charm ◆ Sincerity	◆ Written reproduction of spoken language ◆ Humor and charm ◆ Sincerity	◆ Focused response to the test prompt ◆ Adherence to standard conventions ◆ Formal, academic language
What is remediated	◆ Deviation from formal standard written English ◆ First- and second-person point of view	◆ Skipping any phases of the process	◆ Stiffness of style ◆ Flatness of language	◆ Deviation from formal standard written English ◆ First- and second-person points of view

Writing instruction that improves test performance is not focused entirely on the test. Writers are likely to do their *least* accomplished writing under the artificial conditions of a test. In a test situation, the writers are responding to a prompt that he or she cares little about, if at all. The writers are operating against a time limit that doesn't allow for careful planning, reflection, or revision. The writers are not writing to communicate a real message to a real audience. And the writers cannot do what real writers do, which is write and revise within a community of readers. So let's not think that we can teach *only* toward the test and produce excellence.

Tests are meant to prove that a student has learned enough about writing to demonstrate a certain level of literacy, literacy being a major outward sign of education in our society. But a student's ability to perform for an on-demand writing task should never be thought of as the *goal* of writing instruction. If it becomes the goal, students will never know that writing can be a means for thinking a problem through. They will never know that a first-time-out-of-the-brain "essay" is not the same as a thoughtful, well-crafted *real* essay. A real essay is the result of serious cogitation and recursive attempts to communicate that which may actually not even be consciously known to the writer at first.

The tonic point of this book is that our earnest commitment to produce high writing scores, not only for our students but also for the communities in which we teach, should not override our understanding that writing is a process that is far more deliberative than what can possibly happen in a test situation. The instructional implication of this is that we need to *think outside the test*. We can't get *lost inside the test*.

3

Resistance

As the standardized test movement strengthens, those with objections to standardized testing, and particularly to writing on demand, push back. The National Council of Teachers of English is a notable force in the resistance to widespread, high-stakes tests required by the federal No Child Left Behind (NCLB) act. The NCTE frowns on on-demand writing, believing it to be formulaic and believing, furthermore, that formulaic writing suppresses voice, reflection, and creativity.

A lengthy article in the *New York Times* ("Learn Great Ideas," 2005, p. 8) reported on teacher trainer Nancy Patterson, who runs workshops to improve the pedagogy that would turn students into fine writers about important ideas. But Dr. Patterson laments that the high-stakes test is antithetical to the kind of writing instruction that she is training teachers to deliver. Says Patterson: "If you give kids the formula to write an essay, you're taking away the very thinking that a writer engages in....Kids are less apt to develop a writer's thinking skills....In preparation for the fourth-grade state writing test...third-grade teachers [are] pressed to use the five-paragraph formula."

The resistance to NCLB and the new writing component of the SAT bring forth two phrases that are meant to evoke disdain from educators and the public: "teaching to the test" and "formulaic writing." Both of these are assumed to be bad things, concepts bad enough to have the power to reverse admirable gains in the areas of writing process instruction, critical thinking, problem solving, differentiated instruction, and whole-language pedagogy.

Does the five-paragraph formula really do damage to a fledgling writer's ability to write and think? Is it possible to have a curriculum wherein on-demand and reflective, creative, carefully processed writing are not mutually exclusive? I contend that we can deliver excellent, research-based writing instruction that does not sacrifice the reflective, deliberate thinking required by "slow writing" for the spontaneous thinking required for "fast writing." I contend that instruction for both slow writing and fast writing can mutually support each other. And, in fact, they *have to*: we cannot afford to choose one over the other.

First, let's look at what the research shows us about exemplary writing instruction. Let's see if any of the tenets set forth by the National Writing Project (NWP) and Carl Nagin (2003) stand in the way of teaching students to write on demand for high-stakes tests.

Current research on teaching writing states the following (NWP & Nagin, 2003):

♦ Improving writing is crucial to learning in all subject areas, not just English.

♦ Writing instruction should begin in the earliest grades.

♦ Reading and writing are reinforcing literacy skills and need to be taught together.

♦ Learning to write requires frequent, supportive practice.

♦ Students have diverse abilities and instructional needs, so teachers must use multiple strategies to improve students' writing.

♦ Effective writing instruction pays attention to both the products and the processes of writing.

♦ Writing should be taught in school much as it is practiced by professional writers, that is; students should write for authentic purposes to real audiences.

♦ Students face ongoing challenges in their writing development and need practice with diverse writing tasks to improve.

♦ Simply assigning more writing is not enough: teachers must teach students such skills as how to organize thoughts, develop ideas, and revise for clarity.

♦ An effective writing assignment does more than ask students to report what they have read or experienced. It engages students in such processes as problem solving, reflecting, analyzing, and imagining so that they can think critically about what they have read or experienced.

♦ Schools cannot improve writing without teachers and administrators who value, understand, and practice writing themselves.

♦ Teachers and schools need to develop common expectations of good writing across grade levels and subject areas.

♦ Schools and districts need to develop fair and authentic writing assessments that are aligned with high standards and reflect student progress beyond single-test evaluations.

♦ Effective schoolwide writing programs involve the entire faculty and are developed across the curriculum.

◆ Schools and districts need to offer professional development opportunities in teaching writing to all faculty.

These tenets conflate into a handful of main ideas, as detailed in the next section.

Immersion: Frequency, Persistence, Variety, and Guided Practice

Frequency

Schools that produce strong writers view writing as the centerpiece of instruction. These are not schools where the English teacher is the only writing teacher. Nor are these schools where students write only to be assessed. Because there simply isn't enough time for teachers to assess every piece of writing that students do, students need to be doing a lot of writing that teachers aren't expected to read. For this to happen, students need to write as part of the process of learning, as well as to assess what has been learned.

Persistence

Writing is a developmental skill. If you miss a year, you've missed more than a year's growth because not only have you missed the chance to increase your skills, they will also atrophy. Writing, as a skill, requires stamina that can be built up only through consistent practice. This is why it is a poor idea to have students who have failed English (or another writing-intensive course) double up on their English courses: the student who takes 10th and 11th grade English simultaneously does not improve skills just by doing twice as much work within the same amount of time. Writing improvement is a recursive process, highly dependent on the cumulative nature of prior knowledge and skills that become automatic as they are practiced over time.

Pedagogy and Modeling

It is a truism that we teach best that which we know best. Conversely, we can't teach very well what we do not know. Yet many educators are themselves not good, fluent, reader-based writers. Staff development to improve student writing must address *educators as writers*.

The Role of Reading

Because writing is not speech, writers must be readers. Speaking and listening are extremely important, but only the reading mode of communication provides the cadence and conventions that we need to become writers. It is by reading that we internalize all of those visual cues that pertain only to the written language: capitalization, punctuation, complete sentences, and paragraphs, to name a few. Reading and writing are not separate cognitive processes, and teaching one is teaching the other.

Authenticity

The on-demand writing task on a state-mandated test may seem anything but authentic. The context and the prompt are external to the student's perspective; the audience, seemingly absent. However, the audience should be a presence. To find an authentic (albeit formal) voice, the writer needs to imagine the audience and fill the audience's need. This practice, called reader-based writing, is an essential attitude.

The irony is that the increased emphasis on writing is thought by some of the major players in the writing pedagogy movement to result in instruction that will deliver poorer writing and thinking! The fact is, if you can do something—in this case, writing—well, then you can do it well in a variety of circumstances.

Furthermore, the scorers of on-demand writing take its spontaneity into account. Scorers are trained to look at the piece holistically, even as they are guided by a rubric. They are not reading for mistakes, as would a copy editor. Nor are they expecting an in-depth examination of a complex topic.

Critics of on-demand writing assessments make two false assumptions. The first is that on-demand, formulaic writing will supplant processed, reflective writing. The second is that the latter kind of writing does not prepare the writer for the former kind. In other words, if educators did nothing but on-demand, formulaic writing to prepare students for the test, their strategy would backfire because students wouldn't actually learn to write that way. A school needs to develop writers through a philosophy that posits that writing needs to pervade the learning experience throughout the school day.

In Defense of the Five-Paragraph Essay

Because of its formulaic nature, many educators disparage the five-paragraph essay. They consider it an inauthentic, boxed-in way of writing, more like executing a task than writing something intended to be meaningful. It is true enough that the five-paragraph essay does not exist as a genre outside of school, but it is a format that students, especially weak students, understand and can grow into and out of.

Organization and development are big problems for weak writers. The organization that we teach with the five-paragraph essay facilitates development, providing slots for main ideas and support. Most teachers have found through experience that it's the weakest writers who need the most structure. The five-paragraph essay form solves many problems, not the least of which is volume. Look at an array of student writing samples, from weak to strong. You will undoubtedly find that those on the weak end are seriously underdeveloped, lacking any kind of paragraph structure. You will also find papers, higher up on the scoring guide but still weak, in which the student goes on for two sides of a page without bothering to structure paragraphs. Such a writer is being very hard on a reader—not giving the reader clear signals about units of meaning.

We've all read five-paragraph essays that look like this: *In this composition I am going to tell you about...; My first reason is...; My second reason is...; My third reason is...; In conclusion, now I've told you about...* In every group of teachers I've ever worked with, this kind of writing gets a groan. It's true that we don't prefer to read papers like this, but we need to understand that the student who writes like this is on a continuum of development as a writer. The student needs to learn how to remove the self-as-writer from the ideas themselves.

Let's look at a hypothetical student, Katherine, who is at this stage of development. Katherine is in the ninth grade. She is a serious student, doing what she thinks she is supposed to do when she writes like this. To move to the next level, she has to see models. She needs to know what her alternatives are.

Katherine's teacher wants to break her of the habit of announcing her intention at the beginning of every paragraph. But Katherine needs to see exactly how that can be done for the introduction, developmental paragraphs, and the conclusion. By using visuals like the one in Figure 3.1, Katherine can begin to move away from the stock phrases that she needed at first to focus her on the organizational structure of an essay.

Figure 3.1. Writer Responses to an On-Demand Writing Prompt

Topic: Would you be in favor of paying a $1 lower ticket price at the movies if the movie were interrupted twice for 30-second commercial spots?

Novice	*Intermediate*
In this composition I am going to tell you…	When I go to the movies, I like to forget about real life for a while and just get swept away by the story.
My first reason is…	If movies are going to be like television, I say let's just stay home and watch television.
My second reason is…	I wouldn't mind if they showed commercials before the movie starts because then the story would not be interrupted.
My third reason is…	The director and actors in the movie worked hard to get you to pay attention to the whole thing.
In conclusion, now I've told you…	Commercial breaks in movies are more than just a minor inconvenience.

Looked at for its components, there is nothing wrong with the five-paragraph essay formula. It calls for an introduction that establishes expectations for the reader and an explicit thesis statement. It then calls for three well-developed subtopics, each linked to the previous one with a transition. It calls for a conclusion that hearkens back to the thesis statement. Critics of the form point out that not every topic breaks down into three subtopics. This is true enough, but the subtopics don't have to be "three reasons" or "three examples." The writer can address the opposition in a persuasive essay, establish three fields of view in a descriptive essay, or address three sensory experiences in a descriptive essay. In an essay about a memorable experience, one subtopic could be a description of the experience, the next about its significance, and the third about the events leading up to or following it.

In any case, the five-paragraph essay structure is believed in by many educators. For that reason alone, it is a format that students are familiar with and therefore have prior knowledge on which to build. Think of it as a scaffolding that students need as they progress in their development as writers.

4

Using the Test Itself as a Teaching Tool

Tests can be a teaching tool in two main ways. First, getting students familiar with the test format, time restraints, and overall feel of the testing conditions reduces their anxiety. Second, you can cleverly work critical thinking skills into examining the test.

Managing Test Anxiety

A person experiencing test anxiety during exam time can be affected by lack of sleep, digestive discomfort, shortness of breath, nausea, clammy hands, headaches, jumpiness, butterflies in the stomach, or even full-fledged panic. None of these miserable conditions helps the test-taker perform. Although it is true that an elevated sense of tension can enhance performance, acting as a stimulant and motivator, serious test anxiety muddies the mind. It's worth taking the time to teach students how to manage test anxiety.

The test-taker's best weapon against test anxiety is familiarity. Nervous test-takers need to be familiar not only with the test itself, but also with the testing conditions. Many high-stakes tests take place somewhere other than the classroom in which the material was learned and practiced: in the gym, the cafeteria, or even another school. If possible, take the students to the actual setting prior to the test. If this is not possible, learn all that you can about what the test environment will look like and describe it in detail to the students.

Years ago, when I had some serious surgery, the pre-op nurse described for me exactly what would surround me when I came out of the surgery. I was very nervous as I faced this experience, so I asked a friend who had undergone the same kind of procedure to reveal to me any "surprises" that the nurse may have omitted. I then went on the World Wide Web and found a Website for people just like me. I read their postings over and over again. The time that I invested in these mental walk-throughs was well worth it. Having expectations and images in place reduced my anxiety both before and after the event.

Usually, copies of past high-stakes tests are available for classroom use. If possible, use the actual test itself, not just sample test questions. The less students have to get used to on the day of the test, including finding where the questions are, the more time they will have to get right down to business.

It is important that test-takers manage their time strategically. I recommend that writers make a five-minute plan before they compose. The five-minute plan can be an outline, a list of key words and phrases, a diagram, a T chart, or trial sentences. The important thing is that the students get the sense of what five minutes feels like. I require that students do the five-minute plan before all in-class writings. They need to hand in their plan along with the essay. I may glance at the plan *after* I've read their essay to see where they went wrong or right. Not surprisingly, those with a sketchy plan (that doesn't look like it took five minutes to do) often have correspondingly scant development.

The strategic test-taker doesn't plan on spending equal amounts of time and brain power on every part of the test. The strategic test-taker knows the organization of the test items: Do they become progressively more difficult as you go, or are they in random order of difficulty? How long should it take to complete each short-answer item? How long should I puzzle over a difficult item before moving on with the hope of coming back to it later? How discouraged do I get over difficult questions? How much of my spirit and energy is depleted on what kind of questions? Armed with this self-understanding, the test-taker is in a position to make the most of the allotted time.

Of course, the strategic test-taker also needs to know how the test is evaluated. How much is each item and section worth? Are more points lost for a wrong answer than are lost for leaving an answer blank?

Let's call getting to know the structure of the test "strategic practice" and knowing about *oneself* in relation to the test "reflective test practice." In reflective test practice, the test-taker is using parallel thinking to practice for the test: one line of thinking is puzzling out the actual test questions and writing the essay; the other is reflecting all the while on the test taking itself and how best to maximize strengths to build up weaknesses.

But working test after test in class is boring. Rather than doing that, here are some ways that you can make achieving test familiarity just a bit more interesting:

- ◆ *Matching.* Putting two different issues of the test side by side, highlight all phrases that are similar in the test items and essay prompts in both tests.

- ◆ *Grouping.* Decide on categories that the test items and essay prompts fall into and group them accordingly. Students will settle on different categories. Categorizing is a high-level thinking skill.

♦ *Charting.* Make scattergrams, bar graphs, and pie charts showing the frequency of particular key words in essay prompts.

♦ *Ordering.* Arrange the test items and essay prompts in order of difficulty. This will help students decide how to allot their time.

Make sure that you stress that students still have to read the directions carefully even though they may think that they already know what the questions are going to be. Makers of high-stakes tests, especially those that are based on a state's learning standards, are notorious for changing little but significant demands in the prompt. This is so that we teach guided by the standards, not in blind obedience to the test.

Using the Test as a Basis for Critical Thinking

The problem with "teaching to the test" is that doing so is usually a distinctly uncreative exercise. I believe that education should be sociable, interesting, communicative, and lively. It is possible, with a little imagination, to build critical thinking skills into test-preparation activities. Consider higher-level thinking skills: synthesis, analysis, comparison/contrast, and evaluation. The following are some activities that elevate test preparation by infusing critical thinking modes:

♦ *Synthesis.* Have students create their own version of the test, simulating the test items. You probably know as a teacher that creating a test is an extremely effective and efficient way of learning the information as well as staying focused on it.

♦ *Analysis.* Teach your students the actual state learning standards and have them match the test items to the standards, just as you may have done when you were trained on the standards. If the language of the learning standards is too jargon laden, translate it into language that your students can understand.

♦ *Comparison/contrast.* Your state gives a particular kind of exam. Find exams from another state and compare and contrast. Consider the demands of each test, the kinds of skills called for, the language, the directions, and even the layout. This activity will give the students (and you) perspective on the test. They will see it in a new light. And they will discover universal skills in the standards; in this discovery, they may understand why certain skills and ideas are considered important to our society.

♦ *Evaluation.* Most test-makers provide sample responses to be used by teachers in training. These sample responses are called anchor papers. If you've worked with anchor papers along with your colleagues, you probably found that you emerged with a clearer idea of the task requirements. Why wouldn't students benefit from this process as well? If you do this, you can animate the process by having one student play the role of the writer. Select four or five students to be the panel of judges. Distribute copies of the anchor papers to the whole class. Then role-play the judges assigning grades and giving commentary to the writer.

Using the Test as a Means to Understand Perspective

The test-taker must imagine what goes on in the mind of the test-maker. What is this test-maker likely to think of as the right response or as a well-written essay? To know what the test-maker is expecting, we have to see through that test-maker's point of view.

And what is the test-maker's point of view likely to be? For a multiple-choice question—for example, on reading comprehension—the test-maker wants to see if the test-taker can read closely and discern the main idea from detail, fact from opinion, irony from sincerity, and figurative from literal language. Skillful reading also involves having the flexibility of mind to comprehend words that are used in unusual ways.

For essays, the perspective of the test-makers is that they want to know if the test-taker can write in an academic tone of voice, managing language in a way that characterizes an educated person. That is, they want the writer to show respect for the written conventions of the English language, signs and forms that indicate to the reader that the writer is fit to participate in written communication. As for content, the test-makers are looking for a response that clearly respects the demands of the question. Above all, the test-maker is looking for the writer to show due respect for the test (and its reader).

Here is where the balance between on-demand and processed writing comes in. In processed writing, writers often find their own way just by going through the process. They discover what it is that they want to say and may take a meandering path to get there. But when responding to an on-demand task, the writer is expected to stay focused. These are very different mindsets with regard to what writing is all about. The first is a leisurely Sunday drive (a thing of the past), wherein the journey itself is the point of the journey, the destination unknown. The second is the drive to work, when it is necessary to arrive at a particular place, as well as on time. It's important for students to know and feel that difference, to practice one to achieve the other, and to transition easily from one to the other. The mistake that some educators make is their assumption that on-demand writing will happen on its own if processed writing is the only means of instruction.

Whereas processed writing may be "responded to," on-demand writing is "scored." The former may be seen as formative assessment; the latter, summative. The former views the writer as progressing on a continuum, indeed, as a work in progress; the latter views the writer as a competitor against other writers on the same task, or at least against certain criteria. With processed writing, the communicative circle is completed: the writing gets read and the writer receives feedback. But on-demand writing never completes this circle. The writer feels alienated from the reader, and in fact *is* alienated.

This sense of writer alienation plays out in writing that *looks like* the writer had no idea who the reader was going to be, showing no care and consideration for the reader's needs. The writing can be illegible, fail to observe margins, show minimal development, and disregard conventions. There's a lack of writer's etiquette that should not surprise us; after all, who is the student writing for? An anonymous committee of "graders."

The graders must be humanized. What better way to humanize them than to have students themselves put themselves in the role of graders? Such an exercise, as described earlier, has a lot of power in it to allow the student to see that there is a pair of eyes that will be laid upon this writing-on-demand piece, even though the task is highly artificial.

Summary

Using the test itself as a tool for learning brings the test into balance with processed writing, while at the same time treating it as the specialized experience that it no doubt is. However much we may bristle and chafe at the inauthenticity of testing, particularly on-demand writing, we are obligated to give students every chance to do their best on the test. Only then will we be free to return to more authentic writing experiences.

II

Rhetorical Modes

5

Teaching Writing Through Rhetorical Modes

Because much of our understanding of the world comes through the recognition of patterns, it is extremely helpful to understand how writing topics fall into the following major rhetorical modes:

♦ Narration

♦ Description

♦ Cause and effect

♦ Classification and division

♦ Comparison/contrast

It should be noted that some writing texts condense these categories onto only four rhetorical modes: narration, description, exposition, and persuasion.

Each rhetorical mode accomplishes its own purpose. Each comes with its own structure and language. Most text is organized around a predominant rhetorical mode, supported by at least one secondary mode. For example, narration often partners up with description; definition partners with exemplification.

Teaching writing through the rhetorical modes, which are also called discourse modes, goes way back to Aristotle. However, this paradigm for teaching writing lost its place at the table of writing instruction in the 1970s and 1980s when "process pedagogy" came into favor. Actually, there's no reason why instruction in the rhetorical modes needs to compete with writing process instruction: both can be mutually supportive. The advantage of teaching writing through the rhetorical modes, as we will see, is that once we know what mode we're in, we can build within an existing structure that we already understand.

Karen Gocsik, executive director of the writing program at Dartmouth College, says this about discourse mode pedagogy:

[M]odes of discourse instruction can be used to lead students systematically through a hierarchical system of cognitive functions. In these classrooms, professors develop assignments that progress through the modes, moving students from the personal narrative to the analytical argument, and from simple organizational strategies that are chronological and spatial, to more complex organizational strategies that are more formally logical. In this way, modes of discourse instruction sharpen students' critical and analytical skills.

One additional benefit of teaching writing through modes of discourse instruction: this pedagogy is useful in courses throughout the disciplines. Professors who teach courses in history, geography, and psychology can determine ways that modes of discourse assignments might be made to work in their classrooms. For example, professors in the sciences and social sciences might first require students to describe a behavior or phenomenon, then to explore its causes and effects, and finally to build an argument about that phenomenon. This progression of assignments works extremely well in disciplines that are explicitly concerned with the collection and evaluation of evidence. As students move through this sequence of assignments, they will improve their thinking *and* their writing skills. (n.d., paras. 4–5)

What follows is a close-up of each of the five rhetorical modes and the instructional implications of each for the high-stakes essay.

Narration: Tell a Story

Many prompts, like the following, ask for narration:

An Unusual Day: Write a story about an unusual day. Tell what you expected the day to be like and how it turned into an unusual day.

And for older students:

Evaluate a significant experience, achievement, risk you have taken, or ethical dilemma you have faced and its impact on you.

To write an effective essay in response to prompts such as these, the writer must use narration as the predominant rhetorical mode. The secondary mode will be cause and effect, because the story must lead to some significant realization for the writer. And description is almost always embedded in narration.

To write a narrative essay, the reader needs to think like this:

1. In what order am I going to present my events? Should I begin at the beginning and relate the story chronologically, or should I try something fancier, presenting the end up front and then relating how I came to that point? Should I reveal the significance of the event from the get-go, or should I tack it on to the end?

2. How can I bring the story to life? What visual details should I include? What action verbs will make my story come alive?

3. How should I integrate my own thoughts into the narrative while telling what happened externally?

4. The story is about me, so I'm going to be using the pronoun "I" a lot—maybe too much. How can I minimize the use of "I" so that I'm not using it in every sentence?

5. I'm being asked to tell a story. That means the reader wants my experience, my voice. How an I show that I'm mature enough to appeal to this college, and yet not appear as if I'm trying to sound like a person my parents' age?

College application essays are generally supposed to be around 500 words. For the essay that is based on narration, the writer needs to accomplish the following:

♦ Tell a story that has a beginning, middle, and end. The beginning needs to set the stage (time and place) and the writer doesn't have space for more than a few flashes of descriptive language to do so. The middle needs to use action verbs that drive the story forward and keep the reader interested by giving the sense that events are gathering momentum. The ending has to lead to the cause-and-effect conclusion that imbues the narrative with meaning that answers the question, "So what?"

♦ Integrate plot (the narrative) and the theme (cause and effect).

♦ Use a lot of "chronology" words ("then," "after that," "when," etc.) that orient the reader in terms of time.

♦ Use a lot of prepositional phrases that give the reader information about time and place.

When the reader wants to hear a story, the writer should use a conversational but controlled tone. To achieve such a tone, the writer should employ certain techniques that may not be welcome in more formal discourse. Some of these techniques include the following:

♦ *Use of contractions.* Because many teachers frown upon contractions in academic writing, students sometimes (misguidedly) hesitate to use them. The result can be stiff, distant prose.

♦ *Use of dashes and parentheses.* When the writer sets off certain words and phrases with dashes or parentheses, the result is a rise and fall in pitch that gives personality to the prose. But, like contractions, some of our colleagues may frown upon these "upstart" marks of punctuation, preferring the more traditional colons and semicolons.

♦ *Coordinating conjunctions at the beginning of sentences.* Whether or not student writers should begin sentences with coordinating conjunctions, especially *and, so,* and *but,* is a continuing controversy. Although most teachers still adhere to old rules that say you can't begin a sentence with a coordinating conjunction, professional writers do so all the time and have done so for centuries. But in any case, if there ever is a time when beginning sentences with *and, but,* or *so* is acceptable (and desirable), it would be in the narrative mode, the most informal of the rhetorical modes.

♦ *Stylistic fragments.* Stylistic fragments are sentence fragments that the writer uses deliberately to effect a conversational tone and to emphasize an idea. Stylistic fragments, because they break formal rules, have their own charm and moxie. They invite the readers to loosen their ties.

The narrative mode is in a class by itself, then, because of its informality and personal revelation. Some other college application topics calling for the narrative mode include the following:

♦ First experiences can be defining. Cite a first experience that you have had and explain its impact on you. (University of Pennsylvania)

♦ Tell us a story about yourself that will help us to know you better. Illustrate one or more themes, events, or individuals that have helped shape you. (University of Southern California)

♦ Attach a small photograph of something important to you and explain its significance. (Stanford University)

Breaking It Down

For beginners: Carina, a seventh grader, reads significantly below grade level. Her vocabulary is limited and her writing skills are very weak on the conventions. To scaffold the task of writing a narrative, Carina's teacher suggests that she list simple sentences, rather than attempt to compose paragraphs. She also suggests, "Skip two lines between each sentence. That way, we can add detail later."

For intermediates: Marcos, also a seventh grader, gets the basics of the story down on paper, but his punctuation of dialogue is a mess. To clarify how to use quotation marks to delineate the exact words of a speaker, Marcos's teacher suggests that he translate his narrative into a cartoon, using speech bubbles to indicate the speaker's exact words.

For advanced-level thinkers: Bryant is a seventh grader who has always liked to write stories. His teacher suggests that he play around a bit with the order of events, perhaps attempting a flashback or beginning, as *The Odyssey* does, in the middle, and then using a device such as story-within-a-story to inform the reader of past events.

Description: Sense and Sensibility

The descriptive mode calls for writing about sensory detail. This mode relies heavily on nouns and adjectives. Description is usually an embedded component in narration: people and places must be described so that readers can visualize them. Description alone, however, is a rhetorical mode that is not usually called for all by itself. It is more of a supportive mode. In addition to supporting the narrative mode, description is the supportive mode for comparison/contrast, classification and division, and argumentation.

Nevertheless, descriptive discourse is ubiquitous in every kind of use of language, from advertising to the description of symptoms to your doctor. To be a good describer, you must be a sharp observer open to input from all of the senses, not just the visual. Description operates in two realms: the physical, described through the five senses; and the emotional, described through sensibilities. Sensibilities are values such as caring about others, education, hard work, honesty, and integrity.

The descriptive mode can be called into service to inform, entertain, or persuade. As we describe, we choose language that will convey our attitude about the subject. We've come to use the word "spin" to name the way in which we craft descriptive language for the desired perception that our description will have on others. We say that we've put a "positive spin" or a "negative spin" on a given situation based on the way we've described it.

Description is particularly effective and original when we use figurative language. The use of figurative language can be cliché or sublime. When we speak of figurative language, what comes to mind first is probably metaphor and simile. But another powerful kind of figurative language is synesthesia, the mixing of senses. When Shakespeare speaks of his lover reading his sonnet and "hearing with eyes," that is synesthesia. Figurative language makes prose poetic.

What will happen in a good description is that the writer will create a dominant atmosphere by marshaling words that connote a unified impression. Consider the following document-based question that might appear on an American history test:

> Discuss the changes (political, economic, social) that resulted from conquests of Native American peoples by European peoples during the 17th century.

One writer may choose words that, taken together, evoke a sensibility that condemns the Europeans as enslavers and usurpers who aggressed against indigenous people to violate the sanctity of their homes and ruthlessly destroy them, body and soul. Another may use a different kind of language to glorify the same deeds. Do we use the word "invasion" or "expansion"? "Conquistador" or "explorer"? The skillful writer makes deliberate word choices to direct the reader's response. Description is never objective.

The skillful writer needs to consider these questions:

♦ How can I bring in description to strengthen my essay?

♦ Do I have an opinion about this topic that I want to convey with my word choices? If not, then my descriptions need to be as objective as possible. If so, then I need to carefully choose words that form a team that will play for my side.

A good syntactical choice for the descriptive mode is *cataloguing*. Cataloguing, listing a series in a sentence, bombards the reader with examples. Some writers like to present a cascade of adjectives, which is a great idea as long as each adjective is actually different from the others. Some writers like to throw nouns at the reader, and this can be effective because nouns are examples and examples are persuasive.

To have an impact, the writer must make a conscious decision as to how to organize a description. Is the writing going to be organized spatially? From large, dominating images to smaller details? Light to dark? Background to foreground? Is it going to proceed from one person's point of view? From the familiar to the unfamiliar? The writer needs to consider what assumptions are being made about the reader's mind. Who is this reader, and what does he or she know about the subject? These are considerations that the writer needs to take into account when writing in the descriptive mode.

Writers, then, should look for opportunities to include description, even if description is not specifically called for. Good descriptive writing does the following:

♦ Refers to more than one of the five senses

♦ Marshals details that serve to create a unified impression

♦ Supports other rhetorical modes

Breaking It Down

For beginners: Phylicia isn't getting beyond the broadest of visuals in her descriptions. Her teacher moves her forward by suggesting that she include auditory and tactile sensations in her description and organize the description into background and foreground items.

For intermediates: Arthur, a ninth grader, writes adequately, but without awareness of how action verbs are preferable to linking verbs. His teacher advises a "verb upgrade" wherein he will identify the verbs in each sentence and "trade up" some of those flat linking verbs with lively action verbs.

For advanced-level thinkers: Jin is a ninth grader who is ready to enrich her descriptions with figurative language. Her teacher encourages her to experiment with some of the techniques that she reads in poetry that use synesthesia (mixing of the senses) in description.

Cause and Effect: Explaining How and Why

Also called "cause and consequence analysis," the cause-and-effect mode seeks to explain why changes occur. It is arguably the most common rhetorical mode for the on-demand task. Prompts requiring cause-and-effect responses tend to begin like this:

- Discuss the reasons for…

- Explain why…

- State the impact of…

- What effect did/does _____ have on _____?

- Identify at least one change that resulted from _____.

Accordingly, key words to be used in the cause-and-effect essay include the following:

because	impact	direct	if…then
this is why	affect	indirect	thus
this explains	effect	conditions	therefore
cause	evidence	factor(s)	hence
result	reason(s)	internal	lead(s) to
change	consequence	external	

When presented with a cause-and-effect question, the writer needs to ascertain whether it is the speculative *causes* that are being asked for or the observed *results*. Questions asking for causes may look like this:

- Discuss three causes of World War I.

- How are tornadoes caused?

And questions asking for results may look like this:

- Discuss three results of the Industrial Revolution.

- Discuss some possible results of global warming.

Questions that require a discussion of both causes *and* effects may look like this:

- ♦ Explain the relationship between supply and demand.
- ♦ Explain how barometric pressure affects the weather.

Syntactically, cause-and-effect discourse will employ a lot of complex sentences having subordinating conjunctions. What this means in plain English is that we need a lot of sentences having two parts, with one of those parts being a word that begins with *because, when, consequently, after, since,* and the all-important *therefore.*

To organize a cause-and-effect essay, the writer may choose one of the following patterns:

- ♦ *Significance.* Primary (most significant) causes or results are presented first, followed by secondary (contributory) causes or results.

- ♦ *Chronology.* Immediate causes or results are presented first, followed by causes or results that are further away in time from key conditions.

- ♦ *Strength of connections.* Direct causes and results are presented first, followed by indirect causes and results.

Cause-and-effect essays often partner with argumentation. We often base an argument on the assumption that one thing causes (leads to) a certain result.

Cause-and-effect thinking is easy to find all around us. For sports fans, color commentary and sports journalism abound with speculation and explanation that exemplifies cause-and-effect thinking. Ask students to take notes as they watch a competition or a movie, looking for causes and results of decisions, happenstance, talent, teamwork, or the laws of nature. Ask them to notice the implied or explicit cause-and-effect thinking that advertising presents.

The affect-effect difference is a key spelling thorn in the cause-and-effect essay. These words are easily misused not only because their pronunciation is so similar, but also because they are closely related etymologically, coming as they do from the same root: *fec/fac,* meaning "to do or make." Matters are made more complicated by the fact that although *effect* is usually a noun, it is sometimes a verb; and although *affect* is usually a verb, it is sometimes a noun. I like to simplify things by declaring that *effect* is the noun; *affect,* the verb. I use the memory device of associating effect with the: th*e* (emphasize *e*) *e*ffect. The two *e*s together help me to remember that *e*ffect is the noun.

One way to teach cause-and-effect writing is through timelines. A timeline showing a march of events invites thought about causal relationships. So making a timeline prior to writing a cause-and-effect essay is a useful prewriting activity. Another visual is a wheel, with the key cause or result as the hub, and the contributory elements as the spokes.

When we think about complex social issues, it may not be easy to discern causes from results. We observe coexistent conditions, for example: "Women who are in relationships in which domestic violence is practiced against them have low self-esteem." Is the low self-esteem the cause for their being in such relationships, or is low self-esteem the result of enduring violence from their partners? The exploration of this question is itself an important habit of mind for those who think about social problems.

As we organize the cause-and-effect essay, we classify factors. Do the causes arise from within a structure itself (internal causes), or do they arise from external circumstances? Primary or secondary? Proximal or remote? Proven or unproven? Are results inevitable or coincidental? Positive or negative? Expected or unexpected? Thus the rhetorical mode tdiscussed next, classification and division, is a supportive mode in the cause-and-effect essay.

Breaking It Down

For beginners: Harrison is a very concrete thinker, so cause-and-effect is a difficult concept for him. His teacher encourages him to write sentences that link causes to effects using "because" as the mediating word.

For intermediates: Maddie is ready to advance from concrete to abstract thinking, but she needs scaffolding. With the list of cause-and-effect words (see previous list), she can build sentences and, later, paragraphs, that link causes to effects.

For advanced-level thinkers: As an eighth grader, Ross is on the debate team, so he is used to cause-and-effect arguments. He is ready to classify causes as primary or secondary, and direct or indirect.

Classification and Division: Taxonomy

Most people derive satisfaction from orderliness. When we sort and label things, we make sense of them. We seek to organize things and ideas into generalities (categories) and specifics (examples).

A great deal of academic reading is about classification. A system of classification is called a taxonomy. In earth science students learn to classify rocks as igneous, sedimentary, and metamorphic. Then they proceed to learn about the characteristics and development of each of these categories. Without examples, the categories would be meaningless. Characteristics and examples are basic information. A student who is more advanced learns about subcategories (greater differences within the main categories) and cross-categories (greater similarities between categories). Classification is a way of understanding the world.

Essay questions calling for classification as the primary rhetorical mode often use *describe* or *analyze* as the key task verb:

- ♦ Describe three different kinds of economic systems and explain the advantages and disadvantages of each.

♦ International conflict can be caused by various factors such as border disputes, competition for natural resources, religious hostilities, or conflicting cultural values. Select any international conflict and discuss how at least one of these factors contributed to it.

Key words in the classification essay include the following:

kinds of…	group, grouping
types of…	heading
different	parts
category	sections

Classification essays inform through organization. Questions that call for classification on a science or social studies final exam may look like this:

♦ Discuss the significant causes of World War I.

♦ Describe three kinds of rocks.

♦ Explain how the United States judicial system is arranged.

♦ Explain the stages of life as described in Shakespeare's "All the world's a stage" speech.

♦ Discuss several kinds of challenges that you think will face you as a college student.

A classification essay may be organized chronically, spatially, or by order of importance. The nature of classification makes it easy to arrange in Harvard outline form.

Breaking It Down

For beginners: Beginning writers can get the feel of a classification essay by translating a restaurant menu into paragraphs, using the headings as topic sentences. This task will require transition and variety in sentence structure so that it reads like a paragraph, and not like a menu.

For intermediates: Students will find a lot of classification in their science textbooks because much of science is taxonomy. Intermediate writers can use the headings and subheadings of a taxonomic chapter as topic sentences.

For advanced-level thinkers: Advanced-level thinkers can write classification essays where they have to discern the categories and where they show the interrelatedness among categories. Ask them to classify television sitcoms or *The New Yorker* cartoons into categories, name the categories, and delineate the distinguishing features of each.

Comparison/Contrast

The ability to compare and contrast is arguably the most important of all thinking skills. It's hard to think of a problem that does not require comparison/contrast thinking in its solution. It is through comparison and contrast that we distinguish, discern, and evaluate. Often, we use comparison and contrast to explain a concept that is unfamiliar to the reader. We compare the unfamiliar subject to something that the reader knows about, thus revealing the world by means of comparison and contrast. This is a key means of communication that we use as teachers.

Comparison/contrast prompts come in two types: straightforward and evaluative. The straightforward comparison/contrast prompt simply asks for similarities and differences between two seemingly like or unlike things. The challenge of the task is for the student to find similarities between unlike things and differences between like things. Obvious as this sounds, we need to point out to students that we are *not* asking them to state easily noticeable similarities and differences. The closer that two subjects are related, the more the writer needs to look for differences; the more distant two subjects appear, the more the writer needs to find similarities. The evaluative comparison/contrast prompt asks the writer to make judgments: which of two subjects is better, in your opinion, for a particular purpose? So the writer has to decide *which points* to compare and contrast.

Comparison/contrast prompts may look like this:

- Compare and contrast the skills necessary to play soccer with those necessary to play football.

- Explain why you think you are a good match for a particular college.

- If all practical considerations were held constant, would you prefer to live in a big city or a small town?

- Recommend an advertising campaign for hybrid cars.

Key words in the comparison/contrast essay include the following:

more, less	converge, diverge
greater, fewer	whereas
better, worse	but
similar, different	

The writer of a comparison/contrast essay should take advantage of certain syntactical structures that are perfectly suited for expressing polarities. Semicolons work well for managing comparison and contrast sentences. The writer can use the semicolon as a fulcrum to establish similarities or differences by means of the same kind of sentence structure. This creates parallel structure, and parallel structure is easy to comprehend. Compound sentences joined by *and* are great for illustrating similarities; compound sentences joined by *but* are perfect for illustrating differences.

Summary

A strong schoolwide writing program provides reading and writing experiences in the major rhetorical modes. It is hard to overestimate the importance of being mindful of patterns when we enter text. Knowing the pattern means that a good deal of the work of comprehension (in reading) and construction (in writing) is already done.

6

The Narrative Prompt

In the narrative prompt, the student is asked to write a story. In some state tests, the story speculates on a given picture or scenario; in other state tests, the story recounts a personal experience. When we write in narrative mode, we use description as a strong supportive strategy. So the instructional implications of the narrative prompt are that we must teach students both to understand and replicate story structure, and to enliven their stories with description.

To understand narrative writing, you need to do two things: 1) analyze and replicate the components of story structure; and 2) consider the language style in which stories are told. A story is a highly organized arrangement of information that seeks to involve the reader in something that we'll call "the story world." The story world works like this: the writer invites the reader into a place that the reader can picture and is interested in. In this place lives a character whose fate interests the reader. That character has a burning desire (story goal) that the reader understands and cares about. The character runs into obstacles on the way to achieving the story goal. In negotiating these obstacles, the main character is helped and hindered by others. The character undergoes enlightenment as a result of the events in the story. In the end the reader feels that the story resolves with a sense of wholeness. And that's a story.

So a story must have (at least) the following elements:

- ♦ A setting
- ♦ A main character
- ♦ A story goal
- ♦ Supportive characters
- ♦ Obstacles
- ♦ A resolution

We expect stories to be told in a certain style of language; we call this "story language." Story language is not "memo language" ("Please be advised that there was a prince who lived in a great castle"); nor is it language that depends on Latinate vocabulary ("Once upon a chronological interval, there presided a monarch whose residence was a capacious abode characterized as a castle").

Story language—sentence structure and diction—should be lively, inviting, and relaxed. Because a story is a series of actions, it should rely heavily upon action verbs. But the writer needs to anchor the story to its setting, and this is best done by linking verbs.

In addition to story elements and story language, stories have certain features that writers employ to varying degrees. Some of these features include the following:

- *Dialogue and dialect.* Writers who choose to portray conversation verbatim in their stories call on the sophisticated skills involved in capturing characters' voices. This means using quotation marks and commas or colons to signal speech. It also means adding attributives to the speakers so that the reader can follow the conversation. When we set conversation down in writing, we are free to use sentence fragments, slang, and even spelling variations to mimic dialect. There's nothing wrong with novices employing dialogue, but doing so does incur the risk of making punctuation mistakes.

- *Narrative point of view.* When we set pen to paper to tell a story, we need to make an immediate decision about narrative point of view. The picture prompt suggests a third-person point of view, whereas he personal experience prompt suggests writing from the first-person point of view. One pitfall of first person is that novices tend to overuse "I." This problem can be solved by combining sentences.

  Novices often need to be taught to move away from first person and into third person. In fact, many teachers bang it into students' heads that first person is "not allowed" in academic writing. If your students come to you believing this, or if you preach this line yourself, you will need to redirect students back to effective first-person writing for the personal experience narrative. Writing in first person is not inherently wrong, of course. It is a choice, the appropriateness of which will depend upon the writer's audience, genre, and purpose.

- *Figurative language.* More than any other rhetorical mode, narrative description calls on specialized language for beauty and effect.

- *Nonlinear sequence.* We don't have to tell a story in chronological order. More sophisticated writers may choose flashback, in which the end of the story is presented first and then told in chronological order, taking the reader for a ride that will end up where it started from. Or the writer may begin, as Homer did in *The Odyssey,* in media res, in the middle of things, providing exposition as the story progresses.

♦ *Exposition.* Also called "backstory," exposition refers to events that took place before the curtain opened upon what we see now, bringing the characters to this point in the first place.

The Picture-Prompted Narrative

Eighth-grade students in the state of New Jersey are given a photograph of people engaged in some activity on a place where activity might be happening such as a beach. They are then given the following prompt:

Every picture tells a story, but the stories we see may be different. Look closely at the picture. What story is it telling? Use your imagination and experience to speculate what the story is about or to describe what is happening.

The success of the writer in meeting the demands of this prompt will be the extent to which the writer engages the reader in an interesting story, a story that draws richly from the cues in the photograph. The weak writer might simply describe the picture itself, without truly addressing the prompt, which asks for a story about the picture. I'd like to take you through a model lesson for instruction on this task. This lesson, taught by Mrs. Addams, takes approximately 90 minutes of class time. Mrs. Addams teaches sixth-grade students who need instruction in basic writing skills, especially task awareness and development. Without instruction, weak writers might do the following:

♦ Write little or nothing beyond a description of what the picture looks like. They may speak of the picture as a picture, rather than as the basis of a story. Such a weak interpretation of the prompt may begin with something like this: "This is a picture of a girl waiting for a train."

♦ Overuse dialogue, supporting it with little or no narration that sets the dialogue against the background of a properly established setting and other elements of a story.

♦ Omit conflict. A story is more than description. The essence of a story is that the main character has a thwarted desire, an observation worth noting, or some kind of conflict that is resolved as the story runs its course. If the girl in the story is waiting for the train, and the train ambles down the tracks on time, and she boards the train without incident, we have not heard much of a story.

Strong writers might do the following:

♦ *Open with an intriguing, exciting sentence.* The opening sentence could be an exclamation that starts the story off with a bang. Or it could be a statement of the setting that establishes a clear and inviting image for the reader. Or it could establish mystery, inviting the reader to wonder about the main character.

♦ *Use genuine story language.* Good story writers have close familiarity with the syntax, diction, and cadence of narrative. The story doesn't have to begin with "Once upon a time," but some kind of "story-sounding" language is impressive and gives the writer credibility. Sophisticated storytellers use certain sentence-forming techniques, such as inversions, to signal "story territory." Here are some examples:

- **Inversion:** "In a hole in the ground there lived a Hobbit."

- **Intentional fragments:** "She was not aware of her mistake. Oh, no, not at all. Not at all."

- **Stock story phrases:** "And so it came to pass that…"

♦ *Establish a richly described setting.* Skillful writers might include the time of day and time of year, atmospheric conditions and lighting, and the general ambience of the scene.

♦ *Frame the story in a specific genre.* Because sophisticated writers are readers, they are often good at fitting a new story into an old, sturdy frame. By frame, I mean the set of features of a genre, such as fantasy-adventure, fairy tale, fable, mystery, or even a sitcom structure or news story.

♦ *Use figurative language.* Strong writers are capable of elevating the language of the story with metaphor, simile, and even allusion.

♦ *Employ irony.* The skillful writer might be able to shade the story with the double meaning that comes with the difference between the apparent and the real. When the characters are unaware of something that the readers know, that is dramatic irony.

♦ *Show imagination.* The skillful writer will display a sense of fun and fancy with the story. The characters and setting may be original, inviting the reader into a world that departs from the mundane. Imaginative thought comes through as new combinations, new uses for familiar objects, or unlikely events and circumstances.

♦ *Incorporate pathos into the story.* Pathos is the emotional response that the reader feels from any art form, in this case, literature. A writer evokes pathos by creating believable characters and putting them into circumstances that the reader can relate to. To evoke pathos, the writer has to create a connection between the character and the reader.

♦ *Invoke humor.* A sense of humor in narrative is always welcome and certainly a strong indicator of skill in language. Humor in story writing can be played out in dialogue, incongruity, parody, wordplay, or satire.

♦ *Use symbolism.* Personal possessions, weather, and simple household items can take on symbolic meaning in the hands of a skilled, experienced writer. The best symbols are the most easily recognizable.

I wouldn't blame you for thinking that the above features are far too sophisticated for a student writer to incorporate in an on-demand writing task. Certainly, no one would expect to see all of them, or even most of them, in a single piece of writing. But I include them for your consideration as a collection of tools that can elevate the writing of students who are already reasonably successful. Meanwhile, let's take a look at the basic tools of the trade for responding to the picture-prompt.

What Are We Asked to Do? What's the Task?

Mrs. Addams: "We're writing a story that tells what is happening in the picture. First, let's write a sentence that tells the reader where we are and what it feels like to be there. Use your 'be' verb in the present tense."

Commentary: Mrs. Addams gets the students to begin the story by anchoring themselves to the setting. Students who are uneasy about writing can accomplish this:

It is a sunny day at the beach.

It is a simple sentence, to be sure, but it launches the narrative by inviting the reader into the setting.

Mrs. Addams: "We might want to add detail to our opening sentence. How about some prepositional phrases to tell our reader more about time and place? Don't forget, you can begin your sentence with a prepositional phrase to set the stage."

On Long Beach Island, it is a sunny day at the beach on a Wednesday in the middle of July.

Commentary: Remember that finding a place to begin is a major problem for novice writers. By using simple and familiar language, Mrs. Addams is instilling in her students a habit of mind that will go a long way to their success in the picture-prompted essay. They are now in a position to narrate a story according to the expectations of the genre. What she's giving them is procedure. The more they practice the procedure, the more they will be able to make it automatic.

Mrs. Addams: "OK, great! Now we all have a setting for our story. The next step is to meet the important people in the story. Who is the most important person in the picture? Which person are you most interested in? That person is going to be your main character. Let's introduce him or her to our reader in the second sentence. To introduce the main character, we need to tell what he or she is doing. That calls for an action verb."

A girl uses a toy shovel to dig in the sand.

Commentary: You will be relieved to know that I am not going to go through Mrs. Addams's lesson sentence by sentence. But it is important for you to understand how she's laying the groundwork in the sequence of steps that novice writers should go through in the process of writing a story. Indeed, Mrs. Addams is teaching story writing from a picture prompt *as a process.*

Mrs. Addams: "OK, now let's focus that 'main character' sentence with modifiers. Tell me more about this little girl. What does she look like? How old is she? How is she dressed? What do you see on her face? And tell me more about the tool she is using—that toy shovel."

A little girl around four years old uses a plastic toy shovel to dig in the sand.

Commentary: In these first two crucial sentences, Mrs. Addams's students have applied the writing process on a single-sentence basis. Their prewriting has been the examination of the picture; their drafting has been the first version of each of these two sentences; the revision has been the enrichment of each sentence according to Mrs. Addams's explicit instruction. And she will also spend a few minutes inviting students to read their sentences aloud, thus creating more teachable moments and sentence models. Time elapsed: 20 minutes.

Mrs. Addams: "Well, now that we know where we are and who is there, our story can begin. Our little girl on the beach, digging in the sand with her toy plastic shovel, has to be there for a reason. What is she doing? Why? Your job is to make up a story, using clues in the picture. Use your imagination to create obstacles that our main character—this little girl—must overcome. Give her a reason for being where she is, doing what she is doing. Look carefully at the background.

"A story consists of descriptions and conflict. To write description, we need to write with our eyes, our ears, our fingers, and our noses. What colors and shapes do we see? What voices and sounds of nature or machines do we hear? What textures do we touch? How does that sea air smell? How does the wind feel?

"But a story is more than description. A story must have events—the events give the story a beginning, a middle, and an end. To make the reader interested in the events, there should be conflict.

"We can think of conflict in three ways. People conflict with each other when they want different things and can't have what they each want. People can have conflict with nature: there can be a storm that threatens their survival or disturbs their comfort. And people can have conflict within themselves: they can be confused, forced into difficult choices, undecided. It's the working out of conflict that drives the events of the story. So give this little girl a conflict with someone else, or with nature, or with herself."

Commentary: Mrs. Addams has led the students through only the most basic framework of writing a narrative. Students who are more advanced will benefit from instruction in the finer points of story telling: dialogue and dialect, figurative language, nonlinear sequence, and exposition.

The Golden Five

Mrs. Addams uses the term "The Golden Five" to direct her students' attention to the five traits on her state's rubric. She has a poster of the Golden Five in her room, and her students hear the language of the Golden Five *very* often.

Mrs. Addams: "Let's think about our Golden Five before we start to write."

1. Am I doing what the question is asking me to do? (Addressing the Task)
2. Do I have enough examples and explanations? (Development)
3. Have I organized my ideas into paragraphs and led the reader from one paragraph to the next? Do I have an introduction and a conclusion? (Organization)
4. Do I use the kinds of words and sentences that people like to read in a story? (Language)
5. Am I paying attention to the way I am writing this so that my reader doesn't have to reread or be bothered by careless mistakes? (Presentation and Conventions)

Formative Assessments, Scaffolding, and Teachable Moments for the Narrative Prompt

Stories are everywhere. We learn by means of story, we store information as stories, we visualize and construct reality through stories. Mrs. Addams is constantly looking for opportunities to teach story telling itself by raising students' awareness about the omnipresence of stories. Stories are, in fact, at the heart of human learning. It's impossible to exaggerate the importance of story in how we learn and what we remember.

Actually, as Dr. Renee Fuller points out in "Discovering the Story Engram," every sentence that has an action verb is a mini-story. This mini-story, this zygote of knowledge and reality, is what Fuller calls "the story engram." From that juncture of subject and action verb, we can expand the story infinitely.

Tips for the Story Writer: Directions to the Student

Five-Minute Plan

In your five-minute plan, set up the story:
- Where does it take place?
- Decide on a point of view.
- Who is the main character? (Give your main character a name.)
- Who are the supporting characters?
- What does the main character *want?*
- What challenges does the main character face? (Establish conflict.)
- How is the story resolved?

Story Grammar

You may have heard of the term "story grammar" or "story map" to refer to a visual organizer that lays out the basic outline of a story. By using a story grammar, the writer can frame out the story. Here is a simple story grammar:

The story takes place in_____ on/at _____.

Main character: _____

Secondary characters:_____

_____

Plot: The main character wants _____ but

_____ so

_____.

Making a Good Story Better

Writers at every level can use the following tips to create better stories:
- Create characters that *you* care about. When you care about your characters, when they mean something to you, your readers will care about them, and your story will come alive. Look at the person in the picture. Think of someone you like who reminds you of the person in the picture. Think of a time when you were in a similar sit-

uation. How did you feel? Use those feelings in introducing the person in the picture to your reader.

♦ Bring in multiple senses.

♦ Be specific and concrete. Avoid generalities and abstractions in your story.

♦ Choose energetic verbs.

♦ Model your story after existing stories.

♦ Create small moments. Write with a mental magnifying glass.

Dramatic Scenarios

To create your story, you need to set up a dramatic scenario for your character, the person in the picture. Even if there is no person in the picture, the image in the picture—whether it be a house or a landscape scene—is connected to a person somehow. Here are some dramatic scenarios that may spark your imagination:

First time: The person in the story is in that place for the first time. How might the person feel? Nervous? Excited? Frightened? Determined? Prepared? Self-conscious? What might the person be expecting from this experience? What surprises might await him or her?

Last time: Maybe the person in the story is in that place for the *last* time. How might the person feel? Sorrowful? Wistful? Relieved? What memories might the person feel about this place?

Return: Maybe the person in the story is returning to that place, having been on an adventure or in exile. Many (if not most) stories end with the hero returning home, having experienced another world. On return the hero usually feels different and although the home base itself is the same, the hero feels a sense of strangeness and nonbelonging.

Summary

When we teach the narrative prompt through processed writing, we read many stories as models. To transition from processed narratives to on-demand narratives, students need to go into the task knowing what form of story they are going to write. They won't have time to experiment with different story patterns, perspectives, or language styles. So they have to approach the on-demand task already knowing what kinds of story structures are easiest for them to produce effectively. This can only be determined through practice. Through processed writing, students need to develop the following skills so that they can respond to on-demand narrative writing prompts:

- *Creating a story within a known structure.* A "known structure" is a structure that the reader will recognize as a story.

- *Using story syntax and diction.* Students should be able to implement the kind of words and arrangements of words that suggest that a story, and not an informational test, is being told.

- *Placing the character in the context of a setting.* The character must have a relationship to the setting, and the relationship must have some tension in it to generate the story arc (progression of the character through conflict toward resolution).

7

The Persuasive Prompt

In the persuasive prompt, the student is asked to set forth an argument. The argument is usually about something that students would understand and care about: some aspect of school or community life that affects young people, such as school uniforms, school and home rules, sports, driving issues, and so on. In some states, the persuasive prompt is connected to a quotation. The student is required to interpret the quotation, agree or disagree with it, and use evidence from real life as well as literature to support that opinion.

Although it is certainly possible to make a persuasive argument without being familiar with the formal elements of argumentation, knowing those building blocks can be helpful. Without them, unskilled students can lapse into simply repeating their opinions. And if, as a teacher, you don't know them, you may be missing useful strategies in your teaching toolbox.

An argument begins with a claim that, in the author's opinion, something is true. The claim needs to be stated forthrightly:

- "We should change our national anthem from 'The Star-Spangled Banner' to 'America the Beautiful.'"

- "'The Star-Spangled Banner' should remain as our national anthem."

- "Our national anthem, 'The Star-Spangled Banner,' should remain as our national anthem, but the melody should be adjusted so that more people can sing it gracefully."

The claim is then supported by what rhetoricians call a warrant. A warrant is the connection, stated or implied, that connects the data (facts, statistics, reasons, examples, anecdotes) to the claim. Rhetoricians categorize warrants as follows:

- *Arguments based on generalization.* This kind of warrant links a well-chosen example to the larger group: "Our award-winning choir sounds thin and strained when singing 'The Star-Spangled Banner.'"

♦ *Arguments based on analogy.* Also called "case-based" argument, this kind of warrant for a claim, often used in legal arguments, is based upon a precedent that is compared to the case at hand: "The words to the Pledge of Allegiance have been changed to include the words 'under God.' Therefore, we have already accepted changes to cherished American traditions that ritualize our citizenship."

♦ *Arguments based on signs (clues).* This kind of warrant for a claim is based on the belief that certain kinds of evidence signal certain principles or results. This may also be considered the "Where there's smoke, there's fire" argument: "Our national anthem glorifies our flag, which is a symbol of what America stands for. A national anthem should be about a great symbol of its nation."

♦ *Arguments based on cause and effect.* This kind of warrant is based on linking an existing condition to its assumed cause. The cause-and-effect argument is tricky, because not all related events or conditions have a causal relationship. For example, does a stirring national anthem *cause* a sense of patriotism, or is it the sense of patriotism that causes people to revere their national anthem? Is it the particular national anthem that is stirring, or could that same response be evoked by another song designated as the national anthem?

♦ *Arguments based on authority.* This kind of warrant is based on the assumption that the opinion of a person or institution in authority is sufficient to sway the argument. Of course, the effectiveness or ineffectiveness of an appeal to authority would depend on the *audience's* reaction to the chosen authority.

♦ *Arguments based on principle.* This kind of warrant is based on the assumption that the audience will value a principle, such as, "Hearing the national anthem is an important patriotic ritual that affects how citizens feel about their country." If you accept this principle, then you might be swayed by a statement such as this: "The words 'the land of the free and the home of the brave' are some of the most inspiring words than an American can hear."

In addition to these kinds of warrants for a claim, there are other techniques of argumentation that are accessible to novices:

♦ *Anticipating the opposition.* With this technique, the argument is strengthened by acknowledging and preempting what the opposing side would say. Here are some sentence stems that students can use to set up for anticipating the opposition:

Some people might think_____,
but _____.

Although it can be said that _____
_____,
I think_____.

My opinion may be controversial because _____
_____.

Formal debaters address the opposition in the form of rebuttal. In rebuttal, the debater might offer certain concessions to the opposing
viewpoint, acknowledging the validity of selected points in the opposing argument while rebutting the argument as a whole. The debater might rebut by undermining the opponent's evidence as being
irrelevant to the heart of the issue.

For the student writing a persuasive essay on demand, anticipating
the opposition offers an opportunity to think of ideas for development. It answers the all-important "What else can I say?" question.
By including information that anticipates the opposition, the student shows consideration for another's point of view while weighing and balancing different perspectives before settling on a
personal opinion. This is some higher-level thinking, which will
earn points.

♦ *Semantics.* Many, if not most, arguments rest on how we define key
terms. In the case of the "'The Star-Spangled Banner' as national anthem" topic, the term "national anthem" is clear; however, key terms
of the argument such as "tradition" might be defined in such a way
as to support or refute a particular point of view. A flexible definition
of "tradition" would allow for the changing of the anthem; an inflex-
ible one would rely on "tradition," narrowly defined, as the key reason for keeping the anthem as it is.

Students should be taught to consider how semantics affect their argument. They should be taught to establish working definitions for
key terms early in the essay.

♦ *Anecdotes.* Anecdotes are part of persuasive writing because they humanize and exemplify the issues. The anecdote needs to be tightly
formed and directly focused on the issue. Teach students to draw on
not only their personal experiences but also anecdotes from literature, mythology and folklore, movies, and history to support their
arguments.

♦ *Quotations.* Although the on-demand writing task doesn't allow for
the use of outside resources, if students can think of appropriate

quotations from famous documents, literature, or even movies, they should use them to strengthen their arguments.

- *Strong verbs.* As in all writing, strong verbs make the difference between weak and powerful writing. Here is a list of generic strong verbs that go well with persuasive writing:

build	expand	offer	increase	create
accomplish	develop	strengthen	benefit	profit
succeed	support	improve	grow	prevent

Strong verbs energize language, giving a persuasive essay an upbeat, positive feel.

- *Rhetorical questions.* Orators have long recognized the power of rhetorical questions as a persuasive device. Rhetorical questions not only create interesting variety in sentence types, they also involve the audience, urging them to respond in the way that the writer intends.

- *Appeal to universal values in the introduction.* Universal values include concepts such as the beliefs that everyone has the right to feel safe at home and in the community, that everyone deserves equal opportunity, and that everyone should be free to make choices. Persuasive essays are strong when they establish that the writer's opinion is going to connect to these values, making the world a better place.

The Persuasive Prompt for Upper Elementary and Middle School Students

Although younger children would not be expected to construct complex arguments, they are still often expected to write a persuasive essay. The prompt may draw from their own lives only, or it may require some broader knowledge of the world.

The prompt often asks for a specific number of "reasons to support your opinion." That can be troubling, because a good argument can certainly be based on a single reason. It's artificial and superficial to have to supply a certain number of reasons (usually two or three); however, we will encounter prompts such as these:

> Your teacher has asked the class to vote on having a new special subject for the class to learn about. She has given the class two choices: learning the Spanish language, or learning about airplanes. You will have the new subject for one half hour, two days a week. Write a letter to your classmates persuading them to vote for one of these new sub-

jects. In your letter, give two reasons to explain why you want them to vote for the subject that you've chosen.

Your principal would like to supply all of the students in your school with laptop computers in classrooms. She has asked every student to write a letter to her explaining how having their own laptop to use in school would help them learn. Give two reasons explaining how having your own laptop to use in school would help you learn.

If the prompt directs the writer to a particular reader audience, as these do, students need to be taught how to demonstrate audience awareness. Audience awareness for this kind of task involves speaking of oneself in the first person and addressing the audience in the second person. The writer should acknowledge the audience's interests and needs. The writer should also use a language tone appropriate for the position and age of the audience.

Thesis Statements

Although professional writers don't always pin their essays around an explicit thesis statement, it's a good idea for a student writing a persuasive essay for a high-stakes test to do so. The thesis statement can recommend the specific course of action that the reader is trying to persuade the audience to adopt. It can advocate for a position. Or it can state a preference for one thing over another. The chart in Figure 7.1 shows the difference between weak thesis statements and effective ones.

Figure 7.1. Thesis Statements

Weak, Underdeveloped	Effective, Fully Developed
I believe that we should have more choices in our summer reading.	I believe that having more choices on our summer reading list would result in more students reading more books.
We need a place in the school where we can listen to our iPods and use our cell phones.	If students had a designated time and place to listen to iPods and use cell phones, we could eliminate many unnecessary discipline problems.
Our town shouldn't have a curfew for people under age 18.	Having a curfew for people under the age of 18 is discriminatory, ineffective, and economically unsound.

Transitions: Connective Tissue

In a persuasive essay, it is important to link ideas. Transitions are the words that "guide and glide" the reader from the thesis statement to the main ideas. Poor writers tend to lack transitions from paragraph to paragraph; competent writers tend to lead off paragraphs with stock transitional phrases such as "Another reason…" or "My next reason…." But excellent writers do two things that lesser writers don't: they make liberal use of conjunctive adverbs (as in the folowing text), and they enrich the text with sentence-to-sentence transitions.

Let's call the words and phrases that are used for transitions "connective tissue." We can easily teach that there are three kinds of connective tissue words and phrases:

♦ Coordinating conjunctions

♦ Subordinating conjunctions

♦ Conjunctive adverbs

These three tools are extremely useful in putting together persuasive essays. Because this is not a book on grammar, I'm going to simplify the information and clip the list of coordinating conjunctions to three: *and, but*, and *so*. These three little words create relationships that join elements of equal rank (*and*); that set elements against each other in contrast (*but*); and that establish cause and effect (*so*).

The use of *and, but,* and *so* can and should be taught explicitly as an integral part of how to construct a persuasive essay. Students in the upper elementary grades should have thorough practice in using *and, but,* and *so* to expand sentences.

On a more advanced level, suitable for middle school student, subordinating conjunctions (*because, as, since, although, even though*) can establish contrast or set up cause-and-effect relationships. Subordinating conjunctions are tools that need to be explicitly taught. Some teachers are leery of having students begin a sentence with *because,* fearing that they will get into the habit of writing sentence fragments. However, if we teach that a sentence that begins with *because* has two parts, and if we show copious examples of how this syntax is used in all writing, persuasive writing especially, we've taught students a writing technique that will serve them well.

Middle school and high school students should learn to use conjunctive adverbs to establish more subtle relationships. As their name would imply, conjunctive adverbs are modifiers that also serve to link sentences and paragraphs. Some common conjunctive adverbs are *accordingly, consequently, subsequently, moreover, therefore, otherwise, moreover, whereas, however, therefore,* and *thus.*

Another way of building "connective tissue" within a piece of persuasive writing is the strategic use of repetition. The repetition can be verbatim (a refrain), or the writer may reword the thesis at key points in the piece, just as professional editorialists do. Have students identify moments of repetition in editorials. Doing so will improve not only but their writing, but also their reading.

Core Arguments in Persuasive Essays

Students often find it difficult to think of a context larger than themselves. But when writing a persuasive essay, they need to consider how an issue will affect the larger society. They need to think in terms of the key elements of group living. Below are some general effects that a course of action might have on a school or community:

- ◆ A course of action would lead to a breakdown in law and order.
- ◆ A course of action would diminish individual liberties.
- ◆ A course of action would benefit everyone in a community by
  - Increasing property values.
  - Improving the reputation of the community.
  - Making the environment more attractive.
  - Providing jobs.
  - Making people safer.
  - Making people more sociable.
- ◆ A course of action would improve daily life by
  - Making everyday chores more convenient.
  - Making everyday activities more efficient.
  - Eliminating common annoyances.
- ◆ A course of action would make an individual a better person by
  - Teaching an important life lesson.
  - Making that person more mature and responsible.

General Considerations

Students writing a persuasive essay would do well to take these general considerations into account:

- ◆ Who might benefit? Who might be harmed?
- ◆ What are the costs? Where will the funding come from?
- ◆ How would the individual be affected? How would society be affected?

◆ Does this issue involve a conflict between young people and adults?

◆ Is this a territorial conflict? That is, does it involve the use of shared space?

Persuasive essay topics on controversial issues are likely to involve five kinds of social structures:

1. *Life within a family.* These issues are likely to involve parental rules and the children's desire for independence.

2. *Life in the peer group.* These issues differ from the others on this list because peers don't make official rules and laws for each other.

3. *Life within a school.* These issues, similar to those about life within a family, have to do with rules made by people in authority and opposition to those rules by students who desire complete freedom. Typical topics include the use of unstructured time while in school, clubs and extracurricular activities, sports issues, censorship and limits to free expression, school uniforms, codes of conduct, privacy issues, and homework.

4. *Life within a community.* These issues often involve daily quality-of-life issues such as parking, curfews, recreational areas, and use of local services such as the public library. They often have to do with how young people can offer community service, how they can convince taxpayers to support something of interest to young people, the quality of the schools, and so on.

5. *Life in a democratic society.* These issues, similar to but more fundamental than life within a community, are likely to involve the tensions between civil liberties (the individual) and law and order (society).

Planning the Persuasive Essay

To create the balance between processed and on-demand writing, the writer has to enter the test situation with a mental model of the persuasive essay. Have students use the following procedure repeatedly, so they form the thinking pattern.

Strategies for Writing

1. Identify the focus. Highlight the controversial issue you will write about, and check the format below to be used.

2. Check one format:
   ___ Essay (five-paragraph minimum)
   ___ Letter (include date, greeting, salutation)
   ___ Speech
   ___ Article/editorial
   ___ Narrative (story)
   ___ Other

3. On a separate sheet of paper, write your position. Either support (agree with) or oppose (disagree with) the writing prompt.

4. Brainstorm to identify three reasons that support your position. You may use a graphic organizer to help develop your argument.

5. List three specific supporting facts or details to defend your position.

6. Write your introduction by paraphrasing the writing situation and stating your position as your thesis.

7. Develop each reason into a separate body paragraph, supporting it with facts, details, and vivid language. Use transitional devices between paragraphs.

8. Conclude your writing piece by restating your position.

Topics

In addition to writing about these topics, give students practice in the language of persuasion by having them hold informal conversations, structured discussions, and formal debates.

Social Promotion

Writing situation: In some school districts, if a student does not pass his or her classes, he or she must repeat that grade level. Other school districts have what is called social promotion. Even if a student does not pass his or her classes, that student will be allowed to proceed to the next grade to keep up with students the same age. Your school has decided to socially promote students even if they have failed their classes.

Directions for writing: Write a five-paragraph persuasive letter to your school board AGREEING or DISAGREEING with the decision to socially promote its students. Support your opinion with specific reasons and examples.

Vending Machines

Writing situation: Given the nation's growing concern over the increase of obesity in school-age children, the response of many school boards has been to eliminate vending machines containing junk food.

Directions for writing: Write an editorial for the school newspaper either for or against this action. Support your opinion with reasons, examples, facts, or other evidence.

Summer Reading

Writing situation: Many school districts have implemented a mandatory summer reading program. Supporters of this program believe that it is necessary to stimulate and maintain critical thinking skills, expose students to various genres of literature, and encourage students to recognize literature-to-life connections. However, many people are opposed to requiring students to engage in mandatory reading over summer vacation. Your teacher has asked students to write a letter to the Board of Education explaining their opinion on this issue.

Directions for writing: Write a letter to the Board of Education either supporting or opposing the mandatory summer reading program. If you are in favor of the summer reading program, what benefits can you identify and support? How might critical thinking skills be sharpened through reading? What positive effects does exposure to various kinds of literature have on the reader? What comparisons can you make between literature and your life? However, if you are opposed to this program, explain why. List and discuss the negative aspects in regard to you personally as well as the practicality for the student body as a whole. Take into consideration summer schedules and responsibilities (work, travel); time constraints; and even each student's ability to procure the books. Support your opinion with reasons, examples, facts, or other evidence. Convince the board members, even though they may not agree with you, to take your position seriously.

Community Funds

Writing situation: Your town council has funds available to use in a fashion that would benefit members of the community. The money would be used to dedicate the 5.3-acre tract at Liberty Oak Park for community use. One option presented to the council members is to use the land for a skate park and teen center, which could be used by a large portion of the population. Another option is to build a community swimming pool and tennis court.

Directions for writing: Your assignment is to write a letter to the mayor and council in which you build an argument in favor of the skate park and teen center or the community swimming pool and tennis court. Support your opinion with reasons, examples, facts, or other evidence that show how your choice would benefit the community. Convince the council members that your arguments warrant valid consideration. Use complete sentences, descriptive language, and specific examples to support your opinion.

Friendly Advice

Writing situation (used with *Julius Caesar*): Your friend has just written you a letter asking for advice. His very stubborn and ambitious best friend has just become president of his class and has made some positive changes. He has extended the lunchtime, created a court where students can eat outside, and changed the policy so that both juniors and seniors can drive to school. However, he has made some changes that many students regard as negative. He has had air conditioners installed in each room so school can be held year-round, and he has made a fourth year of math and science a requirement for graduation. Your friend is worried because there is a lot of controversy in his school about the president's ideas, and there is talk of eliminating him. Your friend is writing to you because he is unsure of what to do. Should he tell his friend that people want to eliminate him from power, or should he take the other people's side and help eliminate the president?

Directions for writing: Write a letter to your friend about his situation. Should he tell his friend, the president, that people want to eliminate him, or should he side with the others and help eliminate the president with them? Support your opinion with reasons, examples, facts, or other evidence. Convince your friend that you are giving him sound advice.

School Lockers

Writing situation: Your high school administration has decided to eliminate the use of student lockers. This decision has been made because of the increase of illegal substances and the potential danger of a concealed weapon. Therefore, students will be prohibited from locking up any personal belongings and asked to enter through metal detectors on a daily basis.

Directions for writing: Write a letter to your school administrator supporting or opposing (agreeing or disagreeing with) the use of lockers. Support your opinion with reasons, examples, facts, or other evidence. Convince the administration to seriously consider your position.

Summary

Many high-stakes tests require a persuasive essay on a given prompt. Students should go into the test with substantial experience responding to such prompts, which are likely to be about issues that concern young people in their homes, peer groups, schools, and communities. The key consideration for the persuasive essay is audience: writers need to use the kind of language that makes the audience feel respected to set forth reasons that the audience takes seriously. Therefore, key to teaching for the persuasive essay is to get students to put themselves in the shoes of someone else, usually an adult in a responsible position. Classic rhetorical formats may be useful to students as they craft their arguments. In addition to writing, students should engage in conversation, discussion, and debates about the kinds of controversial issues that they will be expected to write about on the test.

III

Interventions

8

Assistive Intervention That Works to Improve Writing

Working Within the "Teach Me Zone"

No matter how weak or strong a student's writing may be, it's always our job to find a way to move that student *up*. Students will, with instruction, move up *one notch at a time*. To help them do this, we need to understand that writing is a multifaceted skill comprising five elements:

1. The ability to interpret the parameters of a question and deliver an answer that meets expectations (Focus).

2. The ability to provide sufficient detail to satisfy the demands of the question (Development).

3. The ability to structure and form information in a manner that facilitates the reader's comprehension (Organization).

4. The ability to choose the proper diction and syntax for the audience and purpose (Language).

5. The ability to adhere to the conventions of standard written English (Presentation).

The skillful teacher perceives which of these facets is the best springboard for meaningful intervention. In reviewing a student's writing sample, the teacher is not looking to mark down all errors and make negative comments on every single minor or major failing. Doing so only convinces the student that all is hopeless. The perceptive teacher looks for strengths that will form the stepping stone toward growth. I am calling that area in which the student is ready to receive instruction the "Teach Me Zone" (TMZ).

All around us, we are bombarded by stimuli that are trying to teach us lessons. You may attend religious service every week, reading the same prayer and scripture, hearing the same injunctions and words of inspiration. The experience may seem routine. But then all of a sudden, the words to a particular hymn or incantation that you've said hundreds of times make sense to you in a way that they never did before. Suddenly you are ready to act. Those words, although you'd heard them many times before, finally made their way into your TMZ.

No teacher can pinpoint the TMZ in every student every time. But teachers who deliver instruction right where it's needed have developed the teacherly habit of asking these questions in response to student writing:

♦ What do I think is the proximal need of this student? (That is, what do I think this student is capable of learning that would make a difference at this point?)

♦ What terminology is this student likely to understand (or be ready to learn) so that I can explain how to improve?

♦ What interventions can I offer?

Now we'll take a look at some actual student writing samples. I've organized these into four categories:

♦ *Deficient.* The student's writing falls short of communicating meaningful information. Gross deficiencies on any *one* of the five key writing facets can result in the overall piece being considered deficient. However, the usual case is that more than one facet of writing is seriously deficient. We want to find the bootstrap that will pull this student into the competent range.

♦ *Competent.* The student's writing is decidedly unexciting and uninspired, leaving much room for improvement. However, it demonstrates minimal competency for the grade level. We want to make that student excellent at what he or she is already good at.

♦ *Commendable.* The student's writing exceeds expectations in at least one of our key facets. We want to show that student that there's room for improvement in other areas.

♦ *Exemplary.* The overall impression of the student's writing is that it is sophisticated and subtle beyond what we expect of a student at that grade level. These students can present a great challenge to us, as we wonder what we can say to make excellent work even better. Often, the TMZ lies in encouraging the use of figurative language, flexibility in voice, and other rhetorical skills.

Here are writing samples by fourth graders on a timed essay for a state-mandated English language arts test. This prompt is a composite, representing the spirit of prompts for a narrative essay that many states require.

Prompt: Many stories are about mix-ups. Write a story about a mix-up caused by a misunderstanding. In your story, tell why the misunderstanding takes place, explain what happened because of it, and explain how it all worked out in the end. In your story, be sure to make the reader interested by including specific details. Your story may be about something that really happened or something that you have made up.

Group One:
From Deficient to Competent

You are about to read two responses that are deficient because the writers are so vague. In both cases the writers fail to competently deliver on the prompt because they gloss over the nature of the misunderstanding, in effect *telling no story.* They provide no visuals, no characterization, and no details. However, they do adhere to written conventions in an age-appropriate way; and despite gaping omissions, they do evince a rudimentary story structure and organizational plan. We'll call these two fourth graders Theo and Danielle.

Sample Response 1: Theo

Hello. I would like to talk about a story about a boy name Eddie. He had his mix-up, it was about spelling.

One day Eddie came to school. It was like every day. After he sat down he had to do spelling. So Eddie didn't get it so he walked up to the teacher and said, "I don't get this page. The teacher said, "Sit down I'll explain it to you." So when the teacher explained it to him Eddie was very happy. So the teacher said, "Eddie come here anytime.

I just wrote you a story about a boy Eddie and his teacher. Eddie was happy after the teacher explained spelling to him.

Sample Response 2: Danielle

One day my friend Kenna came over and I was trying to tell my mom what me and Kenna did at her house but my mom misunderstood me. First I was talking about one thing then I was talking about another. After a while I got very confused.

Because first I was talking about what we were doing then 10 second later I was talking about something else! So after about 10 times of trying to tell my mom what we did Kenna said I was telling it all wrong. So I told her to tell my mom what we did. Well Kenna told my mom what we did at her house. Also she told it right. I have to ask her how she dose it.

TMZ Instruction

The strategy for lifting Theo's and Danielle's writing skills up one notch by intervening in their TMZ is to get them to employ details that make a story a story. They can be taught the following principle: "When you are telling a story, you need to make the reader able to see and hear what is going on."

The teacher might give the following responses to Theo and Danielle:

♦ "I like the way you organized your stories, but I'm not understanding what the whole story is about. What words and phrases can you use to help me see and hear the characters?" The teacher would elicit a list of descriptive words and phrases applying to the characters. For Theo, that would be Eddie and the teacher. For Danielle, that would be herself, Kenna, and her mother.

♦ "Tell me more about the story. Was it funny? Was it sad? Were there any surprises in it?" Here, the teacher is eliciting a reason why this story is worth telling. Theo and Danielle wrote without awareness that all stories have to have some kind of *emotional* value.

♦ "How am I supposed to feel when I hear the story? Draw a picture of a person's face when they hear the story."

♦ "OK, so now we have descriptions of our characters, and we know how we are supposed to feel when we hear the story. What are some words and phrases that will help us feel that way? Put those words and phrases into the story."

♦ "All stories have a beginning, a middle, and an end. Divide your story into three paragraphs to show the beginning part, the middle part, and the end part." In Theo's case, if he inserts descriptive language and a clear emotional piece into the story, his story could rise to the next level. But in Danielle's case, she would have to create paragraph divisions to reach the next level.

Group 2: From Competent to Commendable

Sample Response 3: Ashleigh

Mom told me to go get something from the store. I went to the store but I forgot the list at home on the table. I went back home but my Mom was at work. Then I could not find the list I looked under my bed my mom's room. I checked downstairs and then I said where is that list? My mom got home and said did you go to the store she said. I said no I could not find the list you put on the table. Then I saw a paper in my moms purse I told my mom can I see your purse. I looked and checked and then I said I found it! My mom said oh I must of put it in the pile of papers. So then me and my mom went to the store.

TMZ Instruction

Two facets come to mind that we think are within Ashleigh's grasp: paragraphing and inclusion of detail. Ashleigh's teacher might use the same words about there being a beginning, middle, and end to a story and teach how these three parts determine paragraph divisions. As for inclusion of detail, the teacher might say, "I want to know more about your story. Tell me more about how you went to the store and realized that you were without the list. What store was it? Did you walk there by yourself? Exactly where were you in the store when you realized that you didn't know what you were supposed to buy? How did you feel, standing there?"

Secondary needs: A glaring mechanical flaw in Ashleigh's story is that she has not marked conversation properly. Another is the common mistake of using the objective case pronoun ("me and my mom") instead of the subjective case pronoun that is called for. This widespread nonstandard manifestation is easily rectified by teaching students to take out the "other person" and then see what is left. Native speakers have no trouble seeing that they would say *I went to the store,* and then extrapolating that usage to "My mom and I...". This effective technique is a linguistic-functional way to teach pronoun case. A rule-based way to teach the same thing is to explain the difference between subjective and objective case pronouns, and then establish that we use the former for subjects. In the sentence in question, the pronouns are in the subject position, thereby calling for the subjective *I* rather than the objective *me.* This particular pronoun habit (use of *me* when *I* is called for) is highly stigmatized and highly common. Therefore, teaching it explicitly and repeatedly is worthwhile.

As for the conversation markers, as long as we are asking students to produce stories, it behooves us to teach them how to mark conversation with quotation marks, commas, and paragraph indentations. This skill takes a long time to teach and requires much practice, probably more practice than the skill is worth. For this reason, I am relegating Ashleigh's disregard of it to a secondary position. I consider it out of her TMZ because I think that at this point in her development, paragraphing and providing visual details are more teachable and more likely to produce significant improvement.

Sample Response 4: Lyle

One time me and my brother were making smoothing with a battery a piece of wire and a piece of tenfoyll. Then our little sister came backe shoping with our mom from the grocery store. Then my sister asked us what are we doing and then we told her and she did not understand what we told her.

Then she went to ride her bike then 2 hours past and it was 12:00 a clock. She came bake and asked what we were doing then we told her the truth and she started to pass what we needed.

Then an other one hour past and we finished it and showed it to the audience of the science fair and we won the grand prize trophy.

TMZ Instruction

Interesting things are happening here, aren't they? In his first two paragraphs, Lyle loses credibility with us because of his very poor spelling of words that we would expect a fourth grader to know. But he then actually *impresses* us by spelling difficult words correctly in his third paragraph!

The story itself doesn't quite hit the mark for the prompt. We're not really seeing a mix-up here, just a lack of understanding on the part of the sister. Lyle's teacher might say this: "You need to say more about why there is a mix-up between you and your brother and your sister. Remember, the story doesn't have to be about something that really happened. You can make up something that your sister might have said or thought that would be funny."

Secondary needs: Once the story is fleshed out, Lyle needs to work on the spelling in the first paragraph, and the *back/bake* confusion in the second paragraph. He also needs to learn to say "my brother and I" rather than "me and my brother." As explained above, if Lyle could learn to "leave out the other person" when deciding on pronoun case, he could select the right pronoun. His teacher could ask: "You wouldn't say 'Me was making something with a battery,' would you?"

From Commendable to Exemplary

To get either of these pieces to an exemplary level, we instruct the writers in five areas: more interesting verbs, more adverbials, more transition, improved diction, and sharper nouns.

More Interesting Verbs

The power of a sentence is in its verb. When we tell a story, we tend to use the same uninteresting verbs (*told, said, gave, had*). If you have students who are steady on the basics, you should build up their verb inventory. Ask them to notice the kinds of verbs that they read in stories, and keep a collection of interesting verbs that they can draw from when they write their own stories.

With more interesting verbs, Ashleigh's piece, without any other corrections, might look like this:

> Mom asked me to go get something from the store. I went to the store but I forgot the list at home on the table. I went back home but my Mom was at work. Then I could not find the list I searched under my bed my mom's room. I checked downstairs and then I called out where is that list? My mom got home and questioned did you go to the store? I replied no I could not find the list you put on the table. Then I spied a paper in my moms purse I asked my mom can I see your purse. I looked and checked and then I exclaimed I found it! My mom said oh I must of put it in the pile of papers. So then me and my mom went to the store.

More Adverbials

Adverbs are single words; adverbials are phrases or even clauses that give the same kind of information as adverbs do. That is, adverbials answer these questions: When? Where? Why? How? To what extent? Prepositional phrases are usually adverbial. If we want students to vary their sentence structures, teaching them to begin sentences with adverbials is the best way to accomplish that.

Here is Ashleigh's piece with adverbials added and existing ones noted:

Last Wednesday, Mom asked me to go get something from the store. After school, I went to the store but I forgot the list at home on the table. Because I didn't know what to buy, I went back home but my Mom was at work. Then I could not find the list so I searched under my bed my mom's room. After that, I checked downstairs and then I called out where is that list? Later, my mom got home and questioned did you go to the store? I replied no I could not find the list you put on the table. Then I spied a paper in my moms purse I asked my mom can I see your purse. I looked and checked and then I exclaimed I found it! My mom said oh I must of put it in the pile of papers. So then me and my mom went to the store.

More Transition

Transitions at the beginning of paragraphs strengthen the sense of organization. Even better organization can be achieved by providing transitional phrases from sentence to sentence within the paragraph. Some good transitions that students might not think of on their own are *that is why, consequently, subsequently,* and *therefore*.

Improved Diction

Simply by replacing certain overused and empty words, students can elevate their diction. Some of the worst offenders include *get* (and all of its forms), *go* (and all of its forms), *said, very,* and *really*. Ashleigh's paragraph is full of weak words. Here is what it could look like with improved diction:

Mom asked me to go buy something from the store. I walked to the store but I forgot the list at home on the table. I returned home but my Mom was at work. Then I could not find the list I searched under my bed my mom's room. I checked downstairs and then I called out where is that list? My mom arrived home and questioned did you go to the store? I replied no I could not find the list you put on the table. Then I spied a paper in my moms purse I asked my mom can I see your purse. I looked and checked and then I exclaimed I found it! My mom said oh I must *of put it in the pile of papers. So then me and my mom drove to the store.*

Sharper Nouns

Finally, think how much better Ashleigh's paragraph would be if she gave visuals—specifics—instead of generalities like "buy something" and "the store." Even the word *table* becomes more interesting when we add whether it is the *kitchen table* or the *dining room table*.

All the previous suggestions for improvement are accessible to the student once they are pointed out as choices for revision. To revise—*to resee*—is to put on stronger eyeglasses and make the piece more vivid and detailed. But if we simply say, "Ashleigh, revise your piece and make it more vivid and detailed," she won't know what to do. With these five simple guidelines, she will be able to go from competent, to commendable, to exemplary.

Differentiated Writing Instruction: Prescriptive Lessons

RxWrite

When you go to the doctor, you expect to receive diagnosis and treatment. It does little good for the doctor to simply give you a bunch of numbers that represent readings on various tests. Your doctor may tell you to develop an exercise routine, to stop eating this, to start eating that, or to fill a certain prescription. If you follow the doctor's orders persistently, your numbers may look more favorable on your next checkup.

When you read and evaluate your students' writing, that is a kind of checkup. If they need improvement (and who doesn't?), it does little good to simply say so. You need to prescribe a course of treatment that is specifically suited to their demonstrated needs.

Sometimes, you see the same needs manifested by the entire class: *everyone's* vocabulary needs expansion; *everyone's* language tone needs to be elevated to a more academic register; *everyone* needs a lesson in citing quotations. But everyone's writing needs are certainly not the same. Some students are still not using apostrophes correctly to signify possession. Some are not writing proper thesis statements. Some are writing summaries rather than analyses. These students need more than just a number on top of the paper, more than items checked off on a rubric. They need a prescription for a lesson that will cure what ails them.

You and your colleagues can access or develop a collection of lessons that will encompass a kind of "writing pharmacy." I call such a collection and the system that assigns and follows through on them RxWrite. My own RxWrite collection is accessible on the World Wide Web at http://www.henhudschools. org/hhhs/rxwrite/home.htm. This collection of lessons is keyed to a rubric that has the five elements that I've set forth in the beginning of this chapter:

1. *Focus: addressing the task.* This segment houses five lessons that help students discern what the prompt is asking them to do. Students are directed to these lessons if they write summaries and superficial responses rather than analysis or explanation.

2. *Development.* This segment contains five lessons that help students supply sufficient reasons, examples, facts, and other supportive information to meet the demands of the prompt.

3. *Organization.* This segment lays out five lessons that help students develop an organizational design before writing and use transitions that guide the reader and facilitate comprehension.

4. *Language: diction and syntax.* This segment has five lessons that help students carefully choose the kind of language (diction and syntax) that the reader expects from a writer in an academic circumstance.

5. *Presentation: grammar, spelling, punctuation, and capitalization.* This segment contains 12 lessons that specifically target some of the most common lapses in the conventions of standard written English.

In every case, the RxWrite student is directed back to his or her own writing sample to improve content or correct errors. The less effective way of dealing with student errors is simply to make note of them on the page and then hope that the student pays attention to what has been noted. Perhaps we ask the student to make corrections on the paper; but RxWrite goes the further step, requiring students to read a bit about their problem areas and then take specific action that is directly related to their most recent writing sample.

RxWrite work is private, easily accessible, quick, and, most of all, focused. I invite you to have a look around the Website, where you'll find a teacher's guide and a student's guide. RxWrite is appropriate for students at grade levels from upper elementary through high school and beyond.

Starting Your Own RxWrite

Although you are certainly welcome to use my RxWrite for your students, you may want to start your own. There are various ways in which you can do this:

♦ You can assemble a low-tech version of RxWrite lessons on paper, rather than online. Simply print off copies of whichever RxWrite lessons you want to use and make them available to students. To help you organize, I suggest sorting the exercises into five color-coded folders, one for each section. Don't feel that you have to supply your class with every single one of the 32 RxWrite lessons. Doing so might overwhelm you and confuse the students. Pick one or two lessons from each section. You can always add more later. The more manageable your paperwork is for RxWrite, the more likely you are to keep it going.

♦ You can assemble your own online collection of prescriptive writing lessons by pulling together your favorite sites through a Website called Filamentality (http://www.kn.pacbell.com/wired/fil/index.html). Maintained by Pacific Bell, Filamentality is an online educational tool that allows you to compose hotlists and Webquests. The former is simply an organization of sites for a specific purpose; the latter is a problem-solving procedure that uses Web-based resources.

♦ If you have your own Website, you can do what I did, writing documents that speak to your students about how to improve their writing in specific areas. Needless to say, this takes considerable work; however, you may want to work with your colleagues to develop a schoolwide collection of prescriptive lessons to improve writing. In addition to the lessons, you can include the style guide of your choice, writing prompts, and links to model papers.

I hope that you won't confuse RxWrite with an ordinary grammar book with exercises in it. The difference is that RxWrite offers concise information and then refers the students back to their own writing. Therefore, the transfer between information and performance is built in. We've all seen how such a transfer is *not* generally made between grammar book exercises and the students' own writing. My frustration with this gap is what generated RxWrite: I wanted students to apply what they learned. I wanted them to read lessons that sounded like me, their teacher.

Students may need to do the same RxWrite lessons repeatedly. As developing writers, they have a lot to learn, a lot to practice. Writing improves unevenly, and as students reach for more sophisticated levels of language and more detailed content, they are likely to need all kinds of support across the array of traits on the rubric. Remember that writing skills are executed simultaneously, but they certainly don't improve all at the same time.

Even if you had only three to five RxWrite lessons, you could offer these to students in response to their papers. You could then provide the follow-through that is usually so lacking in the student-to-teacher writing loop. RxWrite raises awareness for both you and your students as to what specific areas of writing need attention.

Summary

We need to approach student writing with a diagnostic mindset, asking ourselves what might work to improve student writing, rather than just constantly marking off what is wrong with it. We need to think of writing improvement as a very slow and recursive process, having four facets:

- *Practice.* The student creates workable formulas and time management strategies by practicing in simulated testing conditions.

- *Modeling.* By reading and analyzing the strengths of model papers, the student sees exactly what excellence looks like.

- *Patterning.* The student comes to be familiar with the testing situation and task through repeated exposure to it.

- *Prescriptions.* The student is given concise, targeted lessons in areas of demonstrated need.

9

Problem Solvers

The Focus Problem

The most common way that student writers go wrong on high-stakes essay tests is that they don't answer the question. They don't attend to the task verb. The task verbs can be *analyze, explain, compare and contrast, convince, persuade, describe, write a story,* and so forth. To the unsuccessful writer, all these task verbs mean the same thing: *tell about.* When the writer *tells about* rather than *analyzes* or *describes,* the result is the focus problem.

Students need to see models of essays that have focus because the writer has attended to the task verb. What does an analysis look like? What does description look like? Sometimes, the task verb is stated indirectly:

> Suppose that a member of your community addresses the Board of Education with the suggestion that all students complete 25 hours per school year of community service. Would you support this suggestion? Explain your reasons.
>
> Suppose your parents want you to continue taking piano lessons for one more year, and you've decided that you don't want to continue because you don't like to practice the kind of music that your teacher requires. Give several reasons why you should study with a different teacher.
>
> Write a letter to your principal suggesting a new club. Tell why this club would be beneficial and interesting.

In the previous prompts, the student is expected to write a persuasive essay. But a writer without sufficient focus might *tell about* community service, piano lessons, or a new club without regard to the intended audience and the reasons that might be persuasive *to that audience.*

Teaching the Thesis Statement

William Butler Yeats was right: Things fall apart when the center does not hold. Most teachers that I've known who teach essay writing place a high value on a cogent thesis statement. They look for it. Professional editorialists and essay writers do not necessarily compose explicit thesis statements, nor do they follow the maxim that the thesis statement needs to appear as the third sentence in the opening paragraph (after the "hook" and the "link"). However, teachers are within their rights to require an explicit thesis statement, because the absence of one is usually a harbinger of lack of focus.

Especially when responding to a prompt, students who write thesis statements point themselves in the right direction and establish credibility. In schools where students have been accustomed to a great deal of exploratory writing (as opposed to prompt-directed writing), learning the discipline of setting forth a thesis statement subdues the tendency to ramble and amble in the vineyards of thought until something interesting comes along. Unlike journal writing or reader response, prompt-driven writing is definitely structured: the thesis statement is at the heart of the structure.

Most teachers like some artful lead-in to the thesis statement, and therefore like to see a "hook" statement that begins the essay—a statement that romances the reader, an invitational statement that lets the reader know that the writer has something worthwhile to say. The "hook" may be taught as a rhetorical question, or as a statement that begins with the word *imagine* or *suppose.* The hook may present an example, description, or even an anecdote that connects to the thesis statement. The hook may be more than one sentence. Going from the hook to the thesis statement is a "link" sentence. The hook–link–thesis statement sequence does two things: 1) it communicates that the writer is in the zone, observing the expected conventions; and 2) it allows the reader to transition. No doubt, what the reader was doing before reading this introductory paragraph was reading someone else's concluding paragraph and assigning a grade, after some thought and a certain degree of agony or ecstasy. Chances are, all of the essays are in response to the same prompt, and so the poor reader is in the midst of a monotonous job. The hook–link–thesis structure may well be the only opportunity that the writer has to distinguish himself or herself as an individual. That is a grim thought, but let's face it: prompt-driven essays don't give the writer much creative choice, and the hook–link–thesis structure does allow the reader's imagination to make itself known before getting down to the serious business of answering the question.

Here is my colleague, Lenna DiFabio, describing her struggles and successes with getting her ninth graders to write effective thesis statements in response to a prompt for literary analysis:

I was going crazy trying to understand why my ninth grade students struggled with creating a thesis statement in their introductory paragraph. Every student demonstrated confusion, even my strongest writers. Introductions from prior writing assignments were inconsistent: several students listed unorganized details concerning the topic, while others simply regurgitated the writing prompt. To illustrate, numerous essays in response to Ray Bradbury's *Fahrenheit 451* read, "Guy Montag was a fireman who was unhappily married to Mildred. Mildred was obsessed with her Parlor Walls. Montag met Clarisse who was 17 and crazy. Mildred and Clarisse were different…". Clearly understanding the concepts, the students were experiencing difficulty expressing their thoughts coherently. For those who managed to formulate a successful thesis statement, their introduction was underdeveloped. You know, one of those wretched one- to two-sentence paragraphs that evokes an instantaneous involuntary cringe. The "hook" technique was seldom utilized effectively. And if they did "hook" me, my excitement would fizzle out as I read on searching for the framework of the writing assignment. In response to these problem areas, I directed students to RxWrite, a differentiated program designed to specifically target problem areas within students' writing. (As the writing teacher, one diagnoses the problem within the writing assignment and "prescribes" a lesson for revision.) Although students would complete their prescribed lessons, their revisions still reflected a lack of understanding. So I took the practical next step: the mini-lesson. Numerous mini-lessons later, the students demonstrated minimal improvement. Feeling frustrated and discouraged, I assigned the next task, hoping that maybe this time they would get it.

We were in the library researching various aspects of the Elizabethan era for the second research paper of the year in preparation for *Romeo and Juliet.* I supplied every student with an index card. By the end of the second day of research, they were required to submit their tentative thesis statement on the note card for my "Green Go" check of approval. After evaluating 65 note cards, it finally hit me: my students thought that the thesis statement was their introduction. It was clear to me that they did not understand the organization of an introduction. I had a serious problem on my hands, and it screamed for an emergency, back-to-basics lesson.

Here's what worked. The next day, as students entered the classroom, I again handed each person a note card. I announced, "Today, I am going to teach you how to write a successful introduction for your paper. I will provide you with a formula that will ensure winning introductory paragraphs from here on out!" I started by explaining that an introduction had three components: the hook, the link, and the thesis statement (or the main idea statement). Informing the students that their note card was symbolic of their introduction, I focused on the thesis statement first. I asked, "What is your paper about?" I instructed them to write their response in one to two sentences on the last couple of lines at the bottom of the note card. Of course, several students attempted to take the lazy way out by retrieving their note card from the previous day. I persuaded them to rewrite their thesis statement on the bottom of the note card because I wanted them to write their thesis statements in the expected place: the introduction. I modeled my thesis statement at the bottom of the board. It read, "Queen Elizabeth passionately loved fashion, and as a result, her style greatly influenced Elizabethans." As I circulated the room, checking every student's statement, I made a few well-received suggestions. (As a result of individually conferencing and approving statements the preceding day, this task was painless.)

At this point, all writers were confident in their work. Sure enough, one student remarked, "I thought the thesis statement was the first sentence in the introduction!" This is when I informed the students to consider their audience. I asked, "Who are you writing this paper for?" They explicitly indicated that I was, indeed, their audience. With great enthusiasm, I explained that I, their English teacher, not their biology or history teacher, prefer rich, expressive language and insightful connections. I continued to explain with dramatic inflection that I want to be romanced, and "hooked" into their writing. I acted out my typical Sunday, where I am faced with an endless stack of essays, emphasizing the monotony of reading the same boring introduction as compared to discovering refreshing creative introductions where the writer has mentally "hooked" me as a reader. Every time I discussed the technique of "hooking" the reader, I physically dramatized the action, forcing the students to correlate a mental image with the technique.

Next, I provided four strategies for students to use in order to formulate an effective hook. Emphasizing that the "hook" is the first sentence of the introduction, I modeled and explained the following options: starting with a relevant quote, a rhetorical question, an anecdote, or a situation created by starting the sentence off with *imagine.*

Informing students of my strategy of choice for this task, at the top of the board, I wrote, "Imagine you are a seamstress in the 1600s working for Queen Elizabeth." After exemplifying my "hook," I instructed the students to create a "hook" of their own on the very first line of their note card, accentuating its placement. Upon completion, they were asked to raise their hand to seek approval. I couldn't believe it: every writer was engaged, and I couldn't make it around the room fast enough. Joe, a reluctant writer, wrote, "Did you ever wonder why students read Shakespeare every year in high school?" Meanwhile, Krystina expressed, "Imagine cooking a meal for royalty with no electricity." As I circulated the room with encouraging energy, every student, even my weakest writers, received positive and honest feedback.

As positive energy was flowing from everyone in the room, I primed my students with the third and final step to creating a successful introduction. Directing their attention to the blank space on their note card, I discussed the task of linking the "hook" to the thesis statement. Reminding students that revising is a natural part of the process, even for their English teacher, between my "hook" and thesis statement, I wrote, "This powerful ruler demanded a different dress for every new day. Designing, stitching, and sewing a highly decadent, multi-layered gown is no simple task for a dressmaker. One would literally work throughout the day and into the night to proudly meet the Queen's high expectations." Without instruction, students were zealously writing and raising their hands for input. One of my notoriously vocal pessimistic students asked, "How come nobody ever taught us this before?" Wow! I broke through the mass confusion and provided a remedy accessible to every writer despite their talent and ability. When the lesson reached its closure, with tremendous pride I congratulated all my students on writing an impressive introduction while holistically improving their writing skills. This lesson was victorious for all, myself included…and that is what it is all about.

What I love about what Lenna did here is that she identified a problem and literally found space (the note cards) in which to address it. In her instruction on thesis statements, she delivered a condensed version of the writing process itself. The thesis statements that her students composed were like "snow globes," miniatures of the whole essay. The note cards created not only a visual but also a manipulative means to signify the special importance of the thesis statements.

The Sentence Wholeness Problem

A group of words that the writer is putting forth as a "complete sentence" can withstand two tests. The first is that you can add a "tag question" to a complete sentence. A tag question is a two-word question that invites affirmation of the statement, like this:

- You used to live in Hawaii.

    You used to live in Hawaii, *didn't you?*

- I've never been to Hawaii.

    I've never been to Hawaii, *have I?*

- You can ride a bike through sand.

    You can ride a bike through sand, *can't you?*

Native speakers of English can make tag questions with ease. Actually, the grammatical knowledge that is called on to do so is astonishing: you have to transform the noun phrase that is in the subject slot into a (subjective case) pronoun, one that agrees with its verb and is properly singular or plural. Then you have to invert the subject and verb, using the auxiliary to form the tag question. If the statement is in the affirmative, you're going to need to insert the negation, according to English rules, and make a contraction. If there is no auxiliary, you use the present or past tense of *do* as a stand-in. Don't forget the question mark, and you're done!

This simple method will work most of the time to test whether a group of words makes a complete sentence. However, for even more reliable results, there's another test: a group of words that is set forth as a complete sentence will be able to transform itself into a question that can be answered with a "yes" or a "no." Here's how that works:

- You used to live in Hawaii.

    Did you used to live in Hawaii?

- I've never been to Hawaii.

    Have I ever been to Hawaii?

- You can ride a bike through sand.

    Can you ride a bike through sand?

If we use both the tag question and the yes/no question transformation to test whether a group of words forms a complete sentence, we get a sense of what a sentence is that is far more reliable than the "complete thought" instruction. This is because the notion of a "complete thought" is entirely abstract, whereas the techniques presented in this lesson rely on something that is much more accessible to the student: a natural sense of the patterns of the language.

The technique of testing for completeness with tag questions or yes/no question transformations would be practiced internally by the student. This lesson makes that internal practice *external,* visible, and audible to all. Students write their own paragraphs on the board or on flip chart paper. They then physically post their tag questions after each sentence. In Phases 2 and 3 of this lesson, students will test for improperly fused sentences (comma splices or run-ons.) This lesson is generated from the work of Rei Noguchi (1991).

Purpose of lesson: To instill the habit of writing complete sentences rather than unintentional fragments, comma splices, or run-ons.

Rationale: Lack of sentence integrity is one of the most glaring and stubborn problems that deficient writers display. Teachers from the earliest grades give students the traditional definition that a sentence expresses a "complete thought." Given the pervasiveness of sentence integrity errors, we should assume that the "complete thought" definition has not worked to solve the problem.

Note that the "sentence wholeness problem" applies only to declarative sentences. Readers and writers do not have problems, generally speaking, with interrogative, imperative, or exclamatory sentences.

Pedagogical soundness:

This lesson is grounded in several principles of durable learning.

- *Use of authentic text.* Authentic literature is used, rather than the controlled, hypothetical sentences that you'd find in a grammar exercise book. Therefore, students are exposed to the rhythms and patterns of beautiful written language.

- *Reliance on the students' intrinsic knowledge about the English language.* The tag questions and yes/no question transformations ring absolutely true to the ear of the native speaker of English. Given the accuracy of the technique and its ease and naturalness of use, this lesson has an excellent chance of succeeding.

- *Use of visuals and manipulatives.* This lesson leaves students with the image of all the sticky notes stuck all over the student-written text to remind them of the tag question technique for testing sentence wholeness.

- *Experiential learning through discovery.* Unlike the traditional and unreliable method of teaching that a sentence expresses a "complete thought," this lesson allows the students to test out a theory for themselves.

Materials:

Samples of literature appropriate for each phase.

Phase 1:

You will need a series of simple sentences. Simple sentences are sentences consisting of a single independent clause.

Phase 2:

You will need a series that consists of both simple and compound sentences. A compound sentence is a sentence that consists of two or more independent clauses that are joined by a coordinating conjunction. The most common coordinating conjunctions are *and, but, so,* and *or.* Less common ones are *for, yet,* and *nor.*

Your biggest challenge in designing this lesson will be finding appropriate text that meets the criteria of having only simple sentences. Avoid text that includes questions, commands, and exclamations, as these kinds of sentences are not the focus.

Flip chart paper or display board (chalkboard or whiteboard)

Sticky notes

Instruction in Phase 1:
Testing for Complete Sentences

Here is text consisting of only simple sentences. It is taken from *Charlotte's Web,* by E. B. White.

> The next day was foggy. Everything on the farm was dripping wet. The grass looked like a magic carpet. The asparagus patch looked like a silver forest. On foggy mornings, Charlotte's web was truly a thing of beauty. This morning each thin strand was decorated with dozens of tiny beads of water. The web glistened in the light and made a pattern of loveliness and mystery, like a delicate veil.

1. Explain that the purpose of what you are about to do is to understand how complete sentences behave.

2. Ask the students to count how many sentences there are in the passage. Doing this gets them to focus on conventions that mark sentences. Have them circle the periods and the capital letters that follow to imprint the visual image.

3. Explain that everyone is going to apply "the sentence test." The sentence test is that a tag question can be tagged onto the end of group of words to make sure that it is a complete sentence. Once you give ex-

amples of tag questions, students will know what you mean and will be able to make tag questions.

4. Write each tag question on a sticky note and post it at the end of each sentence as you go. This will create a visual that shows how complete sentences work.

Your display board will look like the one in Figure 9.1.

Figure 9.1. Display Board Showing the Sentence Test

The next day was foggy, `wasn't it?`

Everything on the far was dripping wet, `wasn't it?`

The grass looked like a magic carpet, `didn't it?`

The asparagus patch looked like a silver forest, `didn't it?`

On foggy mornings, Charlotte's web was truly a thing of beauty, `wasn't it?`

To go further with this lesson, you could establish that through the tag question you can identify the subject. The subject is what the pronoun in the tag question stands for. Note that a pronoun stands for a *noun phrase*, not a noun, as traditionalists will tell you. In the first sentence, "it" represents "the next day"; in the sixth, "it" represents "each thin strand." The value of being able to identify the subject of a sentence is that it raises our awareness about sentence variety: we achieve sentence variety when we begin some sentences with structures *other than* the subject, as E. B. White does. While we are looking at the display board, we can notice other features of fine literature that can grace our own writing, such as varying sentence length and parallelism created through repetition of grammatical structures.

Here is a more sophisticated example of text that you can use as a vehicle for teaching sentence completeness through the tag question technique. Although the sentences are longer than those in the previous example, they still consist of single independent clauses. This selection is also from *Charlotte's Web*.

> Miles away, at the Arable house, the men sat around the kitchen table eating a dish of canned peaches and talking over the events of the day. Upstairs, Avery was already in bed and asleep. Mrs. Arable was tucking Fern into bed.

The tagged sentences look like those in Figure 9.2.

Figure 9.2. Display Board for More Sophisticated Sentences

Miles away, at the Arable house, the men sat around the kitchen table eating a dish of canned peaches and talking over the events of the day, `didn't they?`

Here, the students can see three well-crafted sentences, the first of which opens with an adverbial of time followed parenthetically by an adverbial of place ("when" and "where" information), and the second of which opens with an adverbial of place. Although these are simple sentences, the first one is enriched by two verbals (words that derive from words but that are serving as modifiers): *eating* and *talking*.

Students are ready to proceed to understanding compound sentences when they get the rhythm and pattern of the tag questions. Phase 1 will help students to write complete sentences as opposed to fragments.

Instruction in Phase 2: Forming Proper Compound Sentences

Phase 2 will help students correct comma splices and run-ons. Although these terms are often used interchangeably, there is a difference. A comma splice is a sentence in which the writer has fused two independent clauses with a mere comma, without benefit of a coordinating conjunction. There are three ways to fix a comma splice:

- *Replace the comma with a semicolon.* This is what you want to do if your independent clauses are either so close in meaning that you want them to be unified into a single sentence, or so close in shape and structure that they go well together side by side and seem to belong in the same sentence.

- *Add a coordinating conjunction along with the comma.* This is what you want to do if you want to specify the relationship between the two independent clauses: *and* signifies that information is coming that comports with what has already been said; *but* signifies that conflicting information is about to be said; and *so* signifies causation.

- *Replace the comma with a period, and capitalize the next word.* This is what you want to do if the first two circumstances don't apply and, on second thought, you decide to give these two independent clauses their own houses to live in.

Many people are under the mistaken belief that *any* long sentence is a run-on. A run-on is a sentence where the writer has joined two independent clauses with a coordinating conjunction but without the benefit of a comma! If either of the clauses is short (some like to go by the arbitrary rule of five words or fewer), then the comma is not necessary. Also, the comma is often omitted when the clauses already contain commas that are near enough to the coordinating conjunction that any *more* commas might cause confusion. To fix a run-on, all you need to do is insert the comma before the coordinating conjunction.

To instruct for Phase 2, you'll need text that has compound sentences in it. Here's text from *The Trumpet and the Swan,* by E. B. White:

> One day, about a week before Christmas, a great storm came up. The sky grew dark. The wind blew a howling gale. It made a whining noise. Windows rattled. Shutters came off their hinges. Old newspapers and candy wrappers were picked up by the wind and scattered like confetti. Many of the creatures in the Zoo became restless and uneasy. Over in the Elephant House, the elephants trumpeted in alarm. Lions roared and paced back and forth. The Great Black Cockatoo screamed. Keepers rushed here and there, shutting doors and windows and making everything secure against the awful force of the gale. **The waters of Bird Lake were ruffled by the strong, mighty wind, and for a while the lake looked like a small ocean.** Many of the water birds sought protection on the island.

Figure 9.3 shows what this selection looks like after applying the tag question technique.

Figure 9.3. Display Board for Compound Sentences

The waters of Bird Lake were ruffled by the strong, mighty wind, `weren't they?`

And for a while the lake looked like a small ocean, `didn't it?`

Look at the bold-faced sentence. Unlike the others, this sentence consists of *more than one independent clause.* It is a compound sentence. As such, its two independent clauses are joined by the coordinating conjunction *and,* along with a comma. When two independent clauses join (properly), we have a compound sentence. The clauses in a compound sentence act as equal partners. It is with compound sentences that you want to add another test: the yes/no question transformation.

To teach this, you would want to first develop in the students an eye for coordinating conjunctions, especially *and, but,* and *so.* (These are the leading culprits in improperly fused sentences.) Have the students circle all instances of *and, but,* and *so* in their drafts. Then, have them determine if there's an independent clause preceding or following the *and, but,* or *so.* They make this determination using the tag question test.

Students should learn both techniques for recognizing independent clauses: tag questions and the yes/no question transformation. However, the tag question alone will clear up most sentence wholeness errors. In the event that a student is still failing to spot and correct fused sentences, train that student to apply the yes/no question transformation in addition to the tag question technique.

Instruction for Phase 3: Complex Sentences, Normal Order (No Comma)

Now we'll move into something even more sophisticated: complex sentences. These will be the simpler form of complex sentences: those in which the main clause comes first, followed by the subordinate clause.

Lest you feel like turning around and going home right now, let me encourage you to stay. It is extremely important for students to learn how to write and punctuate complex sentences. This is because complex sentences are capable of expressing complex relationships in a way that simple and compound sentences cannot. Whereas the clauses in a compound sentence (both independent) act as equal partners, the clauses in a complex sentence (one independent, the other subordinate) act in a master-slave relationship. The latter shows a more sophisticated combination of ideas than the former. Thus, if we want students to become more sophisticated in their writing, we want to *explicitly* teach the skill of writing and punctuating complex sentences.

Whereas compound sentences are joined by a small number of conjunctions, which we call coordinating conjunctions, complex sentences can be joined by many other different kinds of conjunctions. I present these in the following text according to their level of sophistication:

- ◆ *Basic.* These are subordinating conjunctions that are probably already in the vocabulary of elementary school students:

    - Conjunctions of time or place: *when, after, before, as, once, since, until, that, while; where*

    - Conjunctions of condition: *if, once, in case, unless*

    - Conjunctions of reason: *because, since*

    - Conjunctions of result: *so*

    - Conjunctions of explanation or specificity: *how, which, that*

- ◆ *Intermediate.* These are subordinating conjunctions that middle school students may be ready to add to their writing vocabulary, but they probably won't use them unless prompted to do so by instruction and modeling:

- Conjunctions of time or place: *whenever, as long as, as soon as; wherever*
- Conjunctions of concession: *though, although, even though*
- Conjunctions of condition: *as long as, provided that*
- Conjunctions of reason: *as long as*
- Conjunctions of result: *so that*
- Conjunctions of comparison: *as, just as, as if*
- Conjunctions of contrast: *while*

Note that these conjunctions and the ones that follow in the next list are language that children of middle school age would not be likely to use in their casual speech. Therefore, these conjunctions are tools that will be one of the factors that distinguish their casual speech from their formal writing. It is extremely important that we explicitly teach the diction and syntax that transition students from speech to written language.

♦ *Advanced.* Now we come to the conjunctions that are characteristically used in academic discourse. As students come to use these, they will be developing that academic voice that we may or may not want, depending upon the genre. You will see that these are not conjunctions typically used in narrative writing. They are used more appropriately in persuasive genres.

- Conjunctions of contrast: *whereas, however, instead*
- Conjunctions of result: *therefore, consequently, as a result, thus, hence*
- Conjunctions of concession: *nevertheless, at any rate, still after all*
- Conjunctions of addition: *furthermore, moreover, likewise, further*

A plain old complex sentence consists of a main clause followed by a subordinate clause. If the sentence follows in that order, then we don't need any commas. Here is a text sample from *Narrative of the Life of Frederick Douglass*, by Frederick Douglass[1]:

> **I got this idea of how I might learn to write when I was working in Durgin and Bailey's shipyard in Baltimore. There I often watched the ship's carpenters saw the wood and prepare it for use.** They would write on the wood the name of the part of the ship where it would be used. **When a piece of timber was intended for the left side, it would be marked "L."** A piece for the front of the ship on the left side was marked "L.F." One for the aft of the ship—the part to the back—on the right was marked "R.A." By watching them I soon learned the names of these letters

and what they meant when put on a piece of wood. I immediately started copying them and in a short time was able to write these four letters: LRFA. This was my step in learning to write.

The sentences in this passage that contain subordinate clauses (and thus are classified as complex sentences) are shown in Figure 9.4, with their clauses tagged.

Figure 9.4. Display Board Showing Complex Sentences

I got this idea `didn't I?` of how I might learn to write `mightn't I?` when

I was working in Durgin and Bailey's shipyard in Baltimore. `wasn't I?`

There I often watched the ship's carpenters saw the wood and

prepare it for use. `didn't I?`

When a piece of timber was intended for the left side,

it would be marked "R.A." `wouldn't it?`

Note that before the clauses emerge to our eyes, we have to leave aside the subordinating conjunction. Also note that some clauses can actually be embedded inside prepositional phrases. Above, the preposition "of" has the entire clause that follows it as its object! A clause that serves the function of a noun is called a noun clause. It's easy to identify noun clauses (or noun phrases) because they are replaceable with "it" or "they and them." Nouns and pronouns are single words; noun phrases are phrases consisting of a noun and all of its modifiers; and noun clauses are structures that do the work of nouns and that have a subject and verb. You may call nouns, pronouns, noun phases, and noun clauses nominals if you want to. Incidentally, it's good to have that kind of language at your disposal so that you can talk to the students, and they can talk to themselves, about the possibilities of expanding the sentence by adding more modifiers into its nominals—or by adding more nominals, for that matter.

Instruction for Phase 4:
Complex Sentences, Reverse Order (Comma Needed)

Now it's a short hop to the most sophisticated phase of teaching sentence wholeness: the complex sentence in which the natural order is reversed. Remember that the natural order is to have the main clause come first, then the subordinate clause. We have one such sentence in the Frederick Douglass passage (see Figure 9.5).

Figure 9.5. Complex Sentence from Douglass Passage

When a piece of timber was intended for the left side,
(subordinate clause, coming first)

it would be marked "R.A."
*(main clause, set off by a
comma to indicate the
reversal of the natural order)*

These four phases of instruction in sentence combining should take place over time as part of a multiyear scope and sequence. Between each phase, students should have weeks or even months to process the information. First, they should have time to recognize simple sentences in literature. Then, they should produce simple sentences in their own text and apply the tag question technique of checking for completeness. Only when the pattern is firmly established as a mental habit should they move on to sentences of more sophistication.

Advancement:

The most sophisticated, and therefore least used by novice writers, kind of conjunction is called the conjunctive adverb, and professional writers use these in profusion. They are, as the name would indicate, a hybrid of a conjunction (joining word) and an adverb (word that answers when, where, in what manner, or why). Conjunctive adverbs differ from garden-variety conjunctions in that they are movable within the sentence. Also, they can be used to comment on the sentence as a whole, and as such are called "whole-sentence modifiers." In any case, if you analyze the writing of skillful students, you will find conjunctive adverbs that you will not find in the writing of less skillful students. Thus, one of the ways to transform the latter into the former is to explicitly teach and model conjunctive adverbs:

accordingly	hence	nevertheless	then
also	however	next	thereafter
anyway	incidentally	nonetheless	therefore
besides	indeed	now	thus
certainly	instead	of course	undoubtedly
consequently	likewise	otherwise	
finally	namely	still	

Note that the conjunctive adverbs don't necessarily signal the presence of a subordinate clause, although they certainly can. Conjunctive adverbs can introduce, or be inserted into, simple sentences as well as compound or complex sentences.

Another Way to Teach Sentence Integrity: Do It Wrong; Get It Right

When students disregard sentence-marking conventions, it is often because as they write, they focus on their own needs rather than the needs of the reader. The reader needs to have sentences clearly delineated.

One way to develop reader-consciousness is to have to attend to a *particular* convention: in this case, sentence making. Instruct students to write their text with *no end punctuation and no capital letters to signal the beginning of a new sentence.* Then, have them go through and decide, consciously and carefully, where their sentences should end. This technique forces students to attend to sentence wholeness, and it also allows them to see how the lack of proper sentence divisions impedes comprehension for the reader. A variation is to have students mark the boundaries of each other's sentences.

The Comma Problem

I don't know which is worse: the sin of comma omission of or the sin of comma commission. When commas are omitted, the reader may merge words that should not be merged, thus causing a word collision that leads either to misunderstanding that continues through the text or confusion that necessitates rereading. Commas are there to facilitate the reader's job.

But some students (and, alas, some teachers) don't really see the relationship between commas and meaning. They believe comma rules are arbitrary conventions. And if you get your comma rules strictly through grammar handbooks, you're bound to be confused. Who can remember pages and pages of information about commas?

You'll find some 16 or so comma rules in most handbooks. I suggest condensing these into four simple guidelines accessible through the acronym LIES:

- ◆ *L is for lists.* Separate items in a series with commas. Everyone wants to know whether or not to place a comma before the final item in a list. It is considered more formal to do so. Don't forget that lists can be a series of single words, phrases, or even clauses.

- ◆ *I is for introductions.* When an introductory grammatical structure (such as a subordinate clause, prepositional phrase, or whole-sentence modifier) precedes the subject of the sentence, use a comma to signal the subject. The reader needs to find the subject in order to accomplish the essential business of linking the subject to the verb, even though this link is accomplished unconsciously. A refinement of this rule would have the writer omit the comma if the introduction is short or unobtrusive; however, because the comma after introductory information is always acceptable, I prefer to teach students to use it whenever the rule applies.

- ♦ *E is for extra information.* We spend a lot of time teaching when to use or not use commas to set off essential information (restrictive clauses) or nonessential information (nonrestrictive clauses). These terms are difficult to digest. Were they not, we wouldn't have to continually teach when to use commas to set off intervening information. The "extra information" rule works like this: use a comma to set off information that delivers *commentary.* You can take this commentary out of the sentence and the sentence would remain intact.

- ♦ *S is for side-by-side sentences.* By "sentences," we mean independent clauses. These, as we've seen above, need to be marked off by coordinating conjunctions plus commas. The *S* piece of the acronym doesn't work for complex sentences that are presented in the expected order (main clause, then subordinate clause).

The LIES acronym is a little broad. Surely, you can find comma situations that it does not cover, like the one just mentioned. However, LIES is a handy rule of thumb.

Teaching the LIES Acronym

I suggest two ways to train students in the LIES acronym. The first is to have them justify commas that they see in authentic literature and quality nonfiction. The second is to have them insert *no* commas into their own text, and then call commas into service one by one, indicating whether each one conforms to the rule of *L, I, E,* or *S.* (You may have to set aside another category for "other.") When students master the LIES acronym, they can go into the handbook and learn all the rules, if you think that is the way to go.

You might think that it would be worthwhile to have students do exercises in the grammar book, inserting commas in contrived sentences that conform to each of the rules. If you do that, however, don't be surprised if you see no carryover between what students can do under direction in decontextualized sentences and what they do in actual text.

In terms of the reader's needs, it's generally better to omit a necessary comma than to insert an unnecessary one. That unnecessary comma is going to break the continuity that the reader needs to make the sentence whole. Sentences are composed of slots: a subject slot and predicate slot, at the very least. Most sentences have a subject slot, a predicate slot, and some kind of object slot, such as a direct object. As a rule—and this is a reliable rule—we do not insert a single comma between a subject and its verb or a verb and its direct object. I'm simplifying, but you may notice that many novices do insert a comma between these required slots. The result is a break for the reader that impedes comprehension. (Notice that I said that we don't insert a *single* comma between the required slots. If you have an appositive or other intervening structure, then you would of course insert two commas on either side of it.)

The Capitalization Problem

Capitalization is one of the earliest writing conventions that we learn. We learn to capitalize our names. We learn upper and lower case letters at the earliest levels of schooling. Having looked carefully at student writing samples on state assessments in writing (and in the content areas), I've come to the conclusion that gross errors in capitalization are a strong marker of weak writing. In other words, show me a deficient writer, and I'll show you a student who pays little heed to capitalization.

Capitalization can be tricky, but we're not concerned with the more obscure and stylized choices in capitalization here. We're concerned with gross lapses in capitalization that get the reader to think that the writer lacks the most basic of skills. Observance of capitalization conventions is a matter of habit, not critical thinking. Here are five techniques for building the habit of capitalization:

- Expect and demand proper capitalization. Insist that students rewrite their work if the capitalization is careless.

- Expect and demand cursive writing in manuscript form once students have been instructed in cursive writing. Really, the capitalization problem is related to the handwriting problem, as students mix cursive and printed letters.

- Model that you regard capitalization as an important writing habit in the way that you write on the board and post written information in the classroom. Do not post student work that has capitalization errors.

- Address specific capitalization trouble spots:
  - Many students make capitalization errors when writing about geographical features. They are confused about the convention requiring that we capitalize "River" when writing "Hudson River" but we use the lower case when referring to "the river" in a sentence, even when that river is a specific river. Have students write paragraphs that are heavy with geographical features to practice proper capitalization. Ask them to detail travel expeditions, global chases, treasure hunts, and other experiences that would involve places on a map.

- The "geographical features" mistakes are similar to "calendar" mistakes. Adapt the above activities to the calendar.

♦ Practice and reinforce the importance of capitalization by having students write from dictation.

Finally, remember that not all capitalization errors are created equal. Some of the more arcane ones, such as capitalizing words of directionality (north, south, east, west) when they refer to a whole section of the United States are far less offensive than failing to capitalize the first word of a sentence. Because capitalization errors are so highly stigmatized, time focused on capitalization habits is time well spent.

The Handwriting Problem

Because we are not at the point yet when all students have access to computers to write for a test, handwriting counts. First impressions are lasting impressions. The first impression that a reader gets when looking at a student's paper is its overall appearance: length, neatness of presentation, and *legibility*. The purpose of writing is to communicate; when we can't read what's written, the quality of communication suffers. Yet handwriting instruction is not emphasized, especially in the secondary schools. Few secondary teachers know what to do when confronted with moderate to severe legibility breakdowns in student writing.

I would say that the first step to solving the handwriting problem is to acknowledge that the ability to produce legible handwriting is an important skill, not just a personal expression of style. In the professional literature, such as that promoted by the NCTE, handwriting practice languishes in disrepute—denigrated, like worksheets, to the lowly status of "not meaningful" work. Whether disregard for handwriting instruction comes from thinking of it as a mundane concern, or whether handwriting skills go uncorrected out of (misguided) concern for individual expression, I believe that handwriting—letter formation—is a skill that needs attention and can be taught.

Illegibility is a "gateway" problem. I found a very high correlation between poor handwriting and overall poor performance in all aspects of the writing task. This could be for several reasons. Lack of practice may result in lack of fluidity and even pain to the hand, creating an aversion to writing. The writer may blur distinctions among letters to mask spelling errors. The writer may not actually view writing as an act of communication with a reader on the other side, but instead may view it as an isolated task, and therefore not see the need to form letters with consideration for the reader's needs to decode them. The writer may resent the whole experience and simply wish to get it over with. The writer, never having been corrected, may not be aware of the extent of the problem, especially if he or she is developing a distinctive style that may have flourishes that interfere with legibility. Finally, the writer's handwriting may degenerate because of fatigue, a significant factor on a lengthy test requiring an essay.

A student's inability to write legibly may be the telltale sign of hand-eye coordination problems, ADHD, or other learning and fine-motor disabilities that need professional attention. Severe cases may be diagnosed as dysgraphia. Dysgraphic students may also have difficulty lining up numbers and columns in math.

Leaving aside those handwriting problems that require occupational therapy or special education services, many problems result from the entrenchment of poor habits—habits that can be changed with awareness and focus. Here are some common writing habits that diminish legibility:

- Making all letters the same height.
- Superfluous lines and loops.
- Lack of spacing.
- Lack of differentiating between similar-looking letters.
- Lack of differentiating between marks of punctuation.
- Lack of differentiating between upper and lower case.
- Lack of closure of letters, either on the top or the bottom.

And here are some minimal interventions that classroom teachers can implement:

- Turn lined paper sideways to allow for even spacing between letters and words.
- Use graph paper to train students to differentiate letter heights.
- Allow students to skip lines. The more white space, the greater the legibility.
- Address the problem diagnostically. Increase student awareness of the specific problems, as delineated above.

If you work with smaller groups of students in a learning center or resource room setting, you may have time to work on handwriting more intensively, with the following interventions:

- Have students write in the air. Air-writing is an excellent way to practice graphomotor skills.
- Practice writing sentences that include the entire alphabet: "The quick brown fox jumps over the lazy dog."
- Provide a model that students can keep in their binders.

♦ Copy and trace from models, paying particular attention to problem areas (spacing, closure, sizing, differentiating heights, etc.).

Some students print instead of writing in cursive because they believe that their printing is more legible. However, because cursive writing is connective, it is a faster way to write than printing. Some students combine print and cursive, and if doing so doesn't interfere with legibility, we should not object; however, the print-cursive combination often blurs the clarity of lower and upper case letters, leaving the reader to wonder if a word is capitalized or not. If the end punctuation is also ambiguous (such as writing a slash-like structure rather than a clear period or comma), then the reader cannot tell where sentences begin and end. At this juncture, a handwriting problem becomes a sentence completeness problem.

Handwriting instruction has its own social history. At one time, conformity to one particular style (the famous Palmer Method) was expected. Variants, however legible they might be, were discouraged. In the last several decades, in an effort to allow for individual expressiveness, educators have downplayed uniformity in favor of the idiosyncratic development of children's own handwriting. Commendable as this might be, style has triumphed at the expense of substance, as anyone who reads student papers written in longhand will tell you.

Ironically, very few age-appropriate materials are available to help the secondary school student improve legibility. Lacking such materials, I offer the following checklist (Figure 9.6). When you cannot read a student's handwriting, diagnose the problem using the checklist.

Figure 9.6. Handwriting Problem Checklist

I'm having trouble reading your handwriting because

_____ You tend to make all of your letters the same height. Legible letters are of different heights.

_____ You are leaving off or curling up the tails of letters that are supposed to have tails: g, j, p, q, y.

_____ You need to leave more white space between words.

_____ You are not closing up letters that should be closed.

_____ You are adding unnecessary loops and/or lines.

_____ You are making punctuation marks (periods, commas) unclearly.

Write the following sentence three times, tending carefully to the above features:

The quick brown fox jumps over the lazy dog.

The handwriting problems delineated above are likely to be in the writer's control, once their awareness is raised.

Two other related problems are failure to write on the lines and failure to observe margins. Both of these habits have a negative impact on the reader. The writer who fails to keep to the lines on the page should be reminded that this habit conveys a lack of care for the appearance of the paper, creating an uninviting offering for the reader. The writer who writes to the edge of the page does the same thing, giving the reader the impression that the writer is out of control. Both of these seemingly innocuous habits are easy to correct, with the result being worth the small effort.

10

From Speech to Writing

I took a very close, analytical look at the syntax of strong and weak writers as presented in the New York State English Language Arts Assessments. I looked at writing samples from the three benchmark levels: fourth, eighth, and 11th grades. Here is what I wanted to know:

- What *strengths* do our strong writers have that our weak writers don't have?

- What *weaknesses* do our weak writers have that our strong writers don't have?

I found that strong writers evidence a certain skill set, and weak writers evidence not only the absence of that skill set, but a very definite constellation of negative features in their writing.

Here is what strong writers do that weak writers don't tend to do:

- Write intact sentences that conform to pattern of feeding information to the reader that conforms to reader expectations.

- Establish generalities, move to specifics, and then return to the generalities.

- Write with copious prepositional phrases, adverbials, and other modifiers that create visuals and provide detail and dimension within sentences.

- Repeat the key words of the prompt.

- Write compound and complex sentences.

- Write intact sentences.

- Use modifiers to convey detail and richness.

- Indent for new paragraphs.

And here is what weak writers tend to do that strong writers don't tend to do:

- Write illegibly, including ambiguous upper and lower case letters and ambiguously formed marks of punctuation. Notably, periods and commas are both written the same way, as diagonal slashes. Weak writers also write off the lines of the paper, have no margins, form many letters that are indistinguishable from other letters, have needless loops, and fail to differentiate letters by height.

- Spell without a sense of the graphic patterns in the English language.

- Disregard the rules of capitalization.

Looking at the strengths of strong writers and the weaknesses of weak writers, one theme is constant: weak writers don't understand that writing is not speech. The evidence of student writing leads to the conclusion that our priority is teaching students how to unlock the doors of the writing community. Although it is theoretically possible for a student to express well-developed ideas with rich language despite the inability to conform to the writer's conventions, such is rarely the case.

To understand the difference between speaking and writing, I'll use the analogy of walking and driving. Speaking is not writing; walking is not driving. Both walking and driving have the same result: moving you along. But whereas walking is natural to the human body, driving is not, although the experienced, well-trained driver develops muscle memory so that driving comes to feel natural. Driving has all kinds of artificially imposed rules and signals: road signs and markings, licensure, speed limits, and turn signals. To be a driver, you must operate within a world of *symbols. Not so with walking. Walking, like speech, is controlled directly by forces within the walker's body. Driving, like writing, is controlled by many more complicated factors (other drivers, pedestrians, etc.).*

Mainly, driving is done *on the road!* We understand this rule perfectly. That is why we don't drive on the lawn, in a field, in the house, or any other nonroad surface, even though doing so may be exactly what we feel like doing. We observe the rules of the road because we fully understand the difference between walking and driving. But our students don't fully understand the difference between speech and writing. The weaker the writer, the more he or she doesn't observe conventions, and the more he or she inserts features of speech that are not features of writing. The stronger the writer, the more writing conventions he or she observes, and the more he or she inserts features of writing that are not features of speech. Therefore, it is extremely important that teachers of writing understand thoroughly the differences between speech and writing, so that we can move students further along on the speech-writing continuum.

Phonics vs. Graphics

Though both speech and writing are made of language, speech is made of language produced and expressed in sounds (phonics), whereas writing is language produced and expressed in marks (graphics). Accordingly, speech relies upon the cadence, pacing, and pitch of those sounds to animate the language. In addition, in face-to-face conversation, the speaker uses facial expression, eye contact, and gesture to communicate. In place of these expressive tools, writers use textual features: punctuation, boldface or italicized type, tables, charts, pictures, and other visuals that direct the reader to receive the information in the writer's intended way. The instructional implications of the phonics vs. graphics dichotomy are these:

♦ We should be explicitly and constantly teaching that speech is not writing, just as walking is not driving. We should not assume that students already understand that speech is not writing. (How many times have we heard students say, with a shrug, "Well, I just write the way I speak"?)

♦ We should exploit the fact that reading is the means through which we absorb the graphic conventions of writing. Therefore, we need to consciously point out and explain the conventions of spelling, capitalization, punctuation, and other textual features during read-alouds. Think of this as pointing out road signs and markings to a child who will eventually learn how to drive.

♦ Accordingly, as we teach reading, we should teach writing; as we teach writing, we should teach reading.

♦ We should raise students' awareness of those features in speech that do not appear in writing. Many of these features are found in the kind of spontaneous speech-write that students use in online communications (e.g., instant messaging).

Time vs. Space

Speech and writing use time and space differently. Once a word hits the eardrums of a hearer, that word can't be made to disappear. On the other hand, the speaker can deny having said something and can make instantaneous repairs to communication. Writing is crafted: the reader will not read that which has been erased. But writing has a permanence, an undeniability, all its own. And writing becomes something that is possessed by the reader. It can be reread, passed along to other readers, and reproduced.

Speech takes place through time; writing, in a place (on paper, usually). The instructional implications to the time-space dichotomy are these:

♦ We should emphasize that once something is written down and given to a reader, it represents the thoughts and skills of the writer. This is all the more reason to write with care and deliberation, a degree of care and deliberation that is not required of speech.

♦ To continue the walking-driving metaphor, we should teach that "accidents" that happen in the course of walking are (usually) far less serious than accidents in driving. Therefore, we need to "write defensively."

Spontaneity vs. Deliberation

Let's get back to the IM (instant messaging, and, to a lesser extent, e-mailing) language for a moment. IM language is an emergent kind of language that is a true cross between speech and writing. IM language affords the immediate conversational feedback, the back-and-forth exchange of speech, but uses graphic symbols (writing), rather than the voice, to communicate. The opposite of IM language would be oratory. In oratory, the person is speaking, but not spontaneously. In oratory, the communication comes from speaker to audience, and except for group reactions, usually applause or other signals of approval, the communication runs one way only, unlike conversation. Whereas IM language is writing that is much like speech, oratory is speech that is much like writing. Accordingly, IM language uses speech features that are not found in writing, and oratory uses features of written expression (parallel structure, formal rhetorical devices, etc.) that are not commonly found in speech. The instructional implications of the differences between the spontaneity of speech and the deliberation of writing are these:

♦ We should contrast IM language with formal written language. Linguists call such translations "code-switching." It's important to do explicit code-switching from speech to writing so that students come to understand the difference between the two modes of communication.

♦ We should use what students know about the conventions of IM language (and it does have its conventions, as your students will eagerly point out to you if you don't use them) to teach the conventions of standard written English. You will find that students value the conventions of IM language because adhering to the conventions marks the user as a member, an insider. Students, being social creatures, have a sense that language use is important and signifies social status. We need to capture that sense and get students to see it in the light of the language of accepted discourse.

Assumptive Information

In face-to-face conversation, speakers assume that more information is mutually known than writers can assume about readers. Speakers rely on listeners, with their affirmative or negative facial expressions, to give them feedback as to whether they are being understood or they need to clarify. But the writer has to be much more explicit: the reader is receiving the information without the context that the speaker has in conversation. The writer needs to make fewer assumptions about the reader's ability to put the message into its intended context. The instructional implications regarding assumptions about contextual understandings are these:

♦ We should remind the student that the reader needs to be told explicitly what the writer is talking about, much more than a listener would have to be told. Additionally, in academic writing in response to a prompt, the writer already knows that the reader (teacher) knows the facts. Thus, the communication itself is artificial. The writer is thinking, "Of course you already know this information about the causes and effects of building the Erie Canal. Why should I have to tell it to you?" The name of the game here is that as teachers we are *posing* as people who don't know the information, when in fact we're the ones who told it to the kids in the first place! This posturing to create a communicative purpose makes things confusing for some students. That is why it is a great idea to set up an audience *other than the teacher who already knows the information.*

♦ We should explain the reader's needs: "I want to know that *you* know what I taught you about _____. Write your answer as though I don't know anything about it."

Informal Diction and Syntax vs. Formal Diction and Syntax

In speech, if a noun eludes us, we can call it a "thingy," a "whatsis," or a "whatever." We can string endless coordinate structures together with "and." But we can't communicate this way in writing. Readers are fussier than listeners. Readers won't tolerate the writer calling something a "whatchamacallit." Readers demand sentences, most of the time.

Closeness to the Listener
vs. Distance from the Reader

It's an endearing, though inappropriate, quality of young writers, that in their writing they try to be friendly. They begin a book report with the word "Hi!" or a sentence in a lab report with "Well." They may end with an extension of good will to the reader: "I hope you enjoyed this report." Linguists call these little touches "phatic functions." Phatic functions are greetings and leave-takings, chit-chat, and polite expressions of human concern that play an important role in conversation. The child, a human engaging in communication, may (adorably) feel obliged to observe these social customs of speech.

It's not that writing is not a polite medium. It is that the politeness expected from writers comes in the form of manuscript presentation (neatness, margins, spacing) and observance of spelling, punctuation, capitalization, and paragraphing. These are the ways in which writers signal that they care about the reader and want the reader to feel comfortable while receiving the message.

Informal language invites the reader to feel close to the writer. Formal language establishes a distance that the writer thinks is proper. The more academic the writing circumstance is, the more distance must be created. Reader-writer distance lies in the hands of the writer. The writer must not only have a sense of whether the writing task calls for closeness (familiarity) or distance (objectivity), he or she must also know how to adjust language to achieve the desired relationship. Here are the instructional implications:

- ◆ We need to give students opportunities to adjust their language tone to achieve different levels of formality (closeness and distance).

- ◆ We need to delineate writing circumstances (such as bread-and-butter notes) in which an informal, conversational tone would be desirable. Greeting cards can serve as excellent models for both informal and formal language that implies closeness or distance between reader and writer.

From Speech to Writing

Let me clarify that although evaluators on the high-stakes test are trained to look grimly upon writing that looks like "speech written down," as we transition students from speech to writing, we must not make them feel as if we are taking away their speech. To do so would leave them, well, speechless. Writers can only write with the language that they have: our students have oral language. Written language is not better than oral language. It is not more expressive, more rhythmic, or more beautiful. Written language, for reasons discussed above, is more codified than speech, or in any case, its codes are more unknown to those students who are not habitual readers.

I have worked one-on-one with many students, helping them formulate ideas in response to a prompt and then plucking their language right out of the air and nailing it to the page. To do this, I need to encourage them to speak, to converse with me about the prompt. As they speak, I take notes and help them to take notes. The notes become an outline, or a cluster diagram, or trial sentences. And then I help them coax an essay out of their framework. In this way, we go from speech to writing. But we're doing it in a way that respects writing conventions: sentences, spelling, capitalization, and punctuation.

Summary

Students won't necessarily make the leap from speech to writing on their own. We need to explicitly teach the writing conventions and tone that characterize standard written English. We need to do this by explaining what linguists know: speech is one thing; writing, another. Poor writers often remark that they write "just the way they speak," as though there's nothing wrong with doing that. However, there is a lot wrong with thinking of writing as nothing other than "speech on paper," especially on a high-stakes essay test. Indeed, seeing if the student knows the difference between speech and writing is a primary *purpose* of the high-stakes essay. In our society, we value the understanding of that difference. We value it so much that we consider it a key criterion for judging whether a person is worthy to hold a high school diploma. However, emotions and self-esteem play an important role in learning. If in our zeal to teach students to conform to the conventions and tone of standard written English, we ignore their rich store of knowledge about speech language, we miss opportunities to teach them. The best course is to use a contrastive approach, explicitly teaching the differences between the language of speech and that of writing.

11

Language and Error

This chapter is about the nature of error in written English. Much of our work as teachers is concentrated on correcting errors, yet those errors persist. To understand why they do and what we can do about it, we need to understand a few concepts about language and error:

♦ Writing requires a code that differs from that of speech. Familiarity with the code comes from extensive reading in the genre in which writing is expected.

♦ Beginning writers will make errors in the code, just as any novice would when learning a complex system.

♦ The errors (deviations from the code) that beginning writers make give us important diagnostic information. We need to find error patterns that give us insight into how we can help beginning writers learn the code.

♦ It is certainly possible to place too much emphasis on error correction at the expense of the communicative purposes of language. It is also possible to mistake error-free writing for good writing. The latter can be interesting, lively, detailed, and accurate without being the former.

No One Can Write
in Someone Else's Language

No one can write in someone else's language. Students come to us with their language, the language that they use to communicate with their friends and family. That language may or may not be English. If it is English, it may or may not be what linguists call, to give it as much neutrality as possible, "the language of wider discourse." This variant of English is sometimes referred to as "the prestige dialect." Every language has a prestige dialect: the form of the language that is used in legal and business communications and under serious, dignified public circumstances. We may call this form of the English language "standard English" or "edited written English." Some people just call it "school English."

Language identity is an extremely sensitive matter, as you certainly know if anyone has ever corrected your language in public while you were in the process of trying to communicate. A public correction of your language may have caused you slight chagrin or fully humiliated you. Your response to the person who corrected you (unbidden) may have been that you took it in stride, grateful for the correction. Or your response may have been mild annoyance at the interruption. It wouldn't be surprising if you felt resentful at having your language style disrespected. A person's language is deeply connected to that person's identity. Language is intimately related to one's background—ethnically and socioeconomically. There are those who believe that a person who says, "With whom are you going?" is superior in education and social class to one who says, "Who are you going with?" There are others who react negatively to the use of forms like *whom* and *shall* in social conversation, believing such forms to be pretentious.

People who are truly knowledgeable about the nature of language understand that language is a fluid and variable social agreement. The English language, like any language, is always changing. Its rules adapt to social use. With few exceptions (notably *ain't*), widespread use eventually trumps the rules in a grammar book. Grammar book rules change, but they change conservatively, as though they are the last to know about how people actually speak the language.

And language not only changes with time, it also varies in other ways. The English language, like all languages, varies by region. Some regions have a dialect that happens to be disdained. Usually, these are the dialects spoken by dwellers of rural regions or, ironically enough, very industrialized urban regions. Your language style varies because of all kinds of factors: social circumstances, surroundings, and emotionality, to name a few. Just as you probably change into casual clothing when you come home from work, you have casual and formal language.

Casual language is not inherently "incorrect." Nor is it "sloppy," "inexpressive," or "uneducated." Casual language is just as rule-governed as formal language. It's just different—closer to the heart, the hands, and the emotions, whereas formal language establishes more distance between the speaker/writer and the listener/reader. Although formal language is associated with intellectual cogitation, it is no more "connected to the brain" than casual language is. The difference is all in the way society chooses to view language styles.

However, the high-stakes essay test is not a test of whether the test-taker has mastered a regional dialect or the variety of language used informally among friends. It is a test that measures the degree to which the student can communicate in the prestige dialect, using the expected conventions of that dialect.

This is very important: I would like to enlighten people, especially educators, about the true nature of language and about the unjustly harsh condemnation that is shaded upon those who speak a variety of the English language that happens to not be the prestige dialect. I believe that language prejudice is a serious and unfair impediment to many different kinds of minorities, both urban and rural. However, we, as educators, have the duty to transition our students into standard English so that they can use it not only on the high-stakes essay test but also in those circumstances, be they business or social contexts, when that is the expected and respected variety of English. Standard English is a kind of passport. (Actually, all dialects are passports into their own speech communities. But standard English is the particular passport in question for the kinds of tests that we are discussing in this book.)

No one can write in someone else's language. That does not mean that students who speak (and write) in a dialect that differs significantly from standard English cannot learn to shift into standard English. Linguists call such shifting *code-switching.* But for them to do that, *teachers* need to educate themselves about the specific differences between the language that is in their students' lives and that which they want to teach them to use in academic circumstances. Sometimes, we teachers know very little about our students' language. Rather than educating ourselves seriously about their language, we spend *all* of our "English language arts" time inculcating students in the prestige dialect, as if that is the only dialect, and as if that is the inherently superior dialect. Again, although it is true that high-stakes tests hold teachers accountable for transitioning students into standard written English, it is also true that we won't get our students there by pretending that their home dialects *do not even exist.*

Our goal should be to teach language *with* students, not *at* them. We teach *with* students when we think analytically, rather than harshly, about how their oral and written language differ from the form of the language that is expected on the test. We teach *with* students when we acknowledge that language choices are a matter of preferences and style (formal and informal), rather than a matter of intelligence or ignorance. We teach *with* students when we show interest in their home language and when we respectfully teach them to transition to expected conventions of academic language.

In 2003, the National Council of Teachers of English reaffirmed their landmark resolution, "Students' Right to Their Own Language," originally set forth in 1974. This statement, a central tenet of the NCTE, seeks to protect the diversity of the English language while at the same time creating the bridge to what the NCTE calls "written edited American English." The goal is to expand upon, not limit, a student's understanding of language. Let's think of a person's understanding of the English language as English I and English II. The former is the language of the home, the language used among friends, the language of comfort and emotion. English I does not have to be formally taught. English II is the language of school and business, a form of English that may be closely aligned to English I or may have significant differences. The difference between English I and English II must be explicitly taught. When features of English I appear in the written form of English II, those features are considered "errors" (e.g., *gonna, wanna, cuz*). In fact, these are not errors, but variants of the English language.

Do we see English I (the home dialect) in literature? Of course. We see it in dialogue in fiction all the time. The language within quotation marks is often English I, while the language outside the quotation marks, the narration, is usually in English II (the school-and-business dialect). We can use this fact of literature to explain how language varies and how language characterizes the speaker. We can teach students to code-switch from English I to English II by using authentic literature. As the character code-switches from the home dialect to the school-and-business dialect, we can consider what is lost in the characterization and what is gained.

Earlier, I used the phrase "sensitive matter" to refer to the way in which people view their home dialect. I believe that, as teachers, we should avoid the words *correct* and *incorrect* and instead use the words *standard* and *nonstandard*, or even better, *formal* and *informal*. It's really a matter of *appropriateness* or *consideration for purpose and audience*. If you were to plan a luncheon for a group of people, you would carefully consider *their* dining interest, not yours. You would want to make a good impression on them by deliberately matching the details of your service and menu to *their* expectations, wouldn't you? In that sense, writing is an act of hospitality: the writer, like the host or hostess, is offering something in the hope that the reader will be pleased. Certainly, the hope is that the reader (guest) will not be unduly inconvenienced by "error."

The Nature of Error

There are more ways to define "error" than meet the eye. We usually think of "error" as an unwelcome and uninformative deviation from what the reader expects. Are there no capitals to begin sentences? No indentations to signal paragraph divisions? Excessive commas to stumble over? Does the reader have to read the wrong homonym and then mentally adjust, saying, "Oh, yes, the writer means *here,* not *hear.*" These lapses in the writer's attention to the reader's response are annoying to the reader because they usurp the reader's attention without returning any meaning. If the reader happens to be a teacher, then the lapse is particularly annoying because the teacher-reader feels obliged to stop reading and insert a correction.

"Mechanical errors" certainly over-claim the attention of teacher-readers, who feel obliged to note every single one of them. Ironically, teachers don't feel similarly obliged to note every sentence that represents a missed opportunity for more complex syntax that would actually convey more meaning. The result is that many beginning writers sacrifice complexity for correctness, with the net loss—writing that is uninteresting—being unnoticed or only vaguely referred to.

In 1977, Mina Shaughnessy wrote *Errors and Expectations: A Guide for the Teacher of Basic Writing*. Shaughnessy's work with beginning writers at New York City Colleges led her to understand that beginning writers, those who are unfamiliar with the codes of academic writing, should be viewed clinically. In other words, when we read a student's writing, we should be doing so with a mindset that makes us ready to learn about where a student is along the road to "getting" the code. The errors that beginning writers make, said Shaughnessy, are cues to the teacher as to what that writer needs to understand so that he or she can write according to code.

Placing and Prioritizing Errors

As you read a set of papers, ask yourself these questions: What are the errors that are the most important to you? *Why* they are important? Do they interfere with meaning? Do they signal that the writer has not considered that you are a teacher and not a friend? Is the writer causing you to interrupt the flow of communication by having to "make corrections" constantly? Are you unable to make connections within the piece? Are you unable to find the answer to your question? How would you key these errors against the phases of the writing process? For example, spelling errors would be addressed in the editing stage, but the error of weak vocabulary would be addressed in the revision stage and also in the brainstorming stage, as the writer composes a word bank. Errors of organization would be addressed in the outlining stage.

Every teacher has his or her own especially irksome errors. For me, they're the comma splice, the *there/their* confusion, the missed apostrophe to signal a possessive, and the unwanted comma separating the subject form its verb or the verb from its direct object. Another reader might not be bothered at all by these errors. When you grade a standardized test essay, your own "10 Least Wanted" errors may or may not be as deserving of condemnation as you think. As you work closely with a state exam's rubrics, you will come to reconcile yourself to the difference between your own house rules and the official rules of the high-stakes test.

You are entitled to house rules. But you should clearly specify what they are, and you should understand that not everybody is as irked by particular styles as you are (or as *I* am by the omitted apostrophe). It would probably surprise you to know that your colleagues either disregard "errors" that you find offensive or enforce "rules" that you think are not rules. Below are some examples:

♦ *Beginning a sentence with a coordinating conjunction.* The coordinating conjunctions, especially *and, but,* and *so* have long been disdained as second-class sentence-beginners. But that is a condemnation that operates more in the academic world than in the real world of written communications. The fact is, the reasons for beginning not only sentences but also *paragraphs* with coordinating conjunctions are logical and far outweigh the reasons for not doing so. Coordinating conjunctions set up an immediate, clear link between an idea to be presented and that which immediately precedes it. We say that we want students to incorporate transitions to guide the reader, but then we take away one of the best tools for doing so. To begin a sentence with a coordinating conjunction is to adapt a conversational tone, a tone with voice. We say that we want students to write "with voice," but then we are guilty of removing from them the very characteristics that would enliven their syntax. And allowing them to begin a sentence with a coordinating conjunction is one of these.

♦ *Ending a sentence with a preposition.* This is another old-fashioned nonrule. Those who abide by it have probably never really examined it carefully. For example, suppose you wanted to say, "Her birthday gift was everything she ever could have hoped for!" That is an expressive sentence that would get along fine in a narrative. Suppose we were to recast this sentence to avoid the sentence-ending preposition, like this: "Her birthday gift was everything for which she ever could have hoped!" That iteration, so stiff and formal, expresses a whole different—and I'd say less effective—voice. While it is true that the sentences that we create when we are deliberately avoiding the sentence-ending preposition are more formal, two things must be considered: 1) formal is not necessarily better; and 2) the cure for the sentence-ending preposition is often much worse than the disease. It's safe to say that the injunction against ending a sentence with a preposition, like the one against beginning a sentence with a coordinating conjunction, is not widely agreed upon and is generally disregarded in professional writing in most genres.

♦ *Writing an essay in the first person.* There's no reason why essays should not use the first person, as long as the writer maintains focus on the question. Beginning writers often believe that everything they write is supposed to give their opinion, and that is why teachers warn against writing in the first person. Also, first-person point of view can sound unacademic. However, the cure is once again often worse than the disease, as the novice who attempts to avoid the first person may sacrifice conciseness and clarity to do so. I think of the first-person point of view as a handy tool that writers use to get themselves through the doorways of the question.

First-person writing is widely frowned upon in essay responses for social studies and science. It is up to these teachers to show beginning writers exactly how to answer the question without using first person.

♦ *Addressing the reader (generally or specifically) in the second person.* Likewise, using the second person to refer to humankind in general, or to the reader in specific, is not usually welcome in academic writing. However, the use of "one" to refer to the generic person is often obtrusive and unskillfully used by the novice. I favor the minimized use of "you" rather than the overuse of "one." Again, if you use models, you can show beginning writers the voice that you want.

♦ *Employing stylistic fragments.* Stylistic fragments are a hallmark of voiced, conversational, inviting writing. However, that is not the kind of voice that we are looking for in academic testing situations. Only the most skilled writers, the ones who have established credibility in other areas of the essay, can get away with stylistic fragments. Stylistic fragments are to writing what casual Fridays are to the workplace: allowable only by special permission.

♦ *Having an implied main idea, rather than an explicit thesis statement.* Here again is something that we see all the time in professional writing. Pick up the editorial page, or any collection of literary writings, and you will not find explicit thesis statements placed where teachers have said they must be placed, at the end of the opening paragraph. You will find many pieces that have implied thesis statements, rather than explicit ones. And you will also find a great deal of repetition (restatement) of the thesis statement.

♦ *Having an implied main idea, rather than a topic sentence in each paragraph.* Except in the most artless prose, such as that which you'd find in an informational textbook, you won't find explicit topic sentences leading off each paragraph in professional writing. But here again, we ask students to write this way so that they stay focused on the prompt and so that we can easily follow their organizational plan.

♦ *Writing one-sentence paragraphs.* The one-sentence paragraph is very common in editorials, where the paragraphs tend to be short anyway. Teachers tend to dislike the one-sentence paragraph because, by definition, it does not supply sufficient reasons and examples for a topic sentence (which, also by definition, it does not have). One-sentence paragraphs, like short sentences nestled amid long sentences, emphasize their (single) ideas.

♦ *Irregardless, anyways, hopefully, different than, the reason is because, have got.* These are informal words and expressions. They are not "wrong" in the sense that their meaning is unclear. However, they are not accorded high status and are easily avoided in academic writing, where their use can diminish the credibility of the writer.

Effective Responses to Errors

Remember that the high-stakes essay is nothing more than a rough draft. Most scoring guides demand that you pay more attention to meaning than to surface transgressions and lapses in proofreading. In the hurry of producing text, *any* writer makes unconscious mistakes that the writer would correct upon careful proofreading. When you evaluate student writing on a high-stakes test, you are obliged to forgo your own personal opinions on the degree of offensiveness of specific expressions and fall into line with how the anchor papers are graded. This adjustment should rightly be jarring to you, and should lead to enlightening conversations with your colleagues about what is acceptable and what is not. Such conversations, if you engage in them with an open mind, will make you a better teacher within the context of your school, a school in which you are not the child's only teacher.

Accordingly, teach students to set up a hierarchy: not all errors (or *variants,* if you will) are equally offensive to all readers. The hierarchy of errors should correspond to the values expressed in the rubric, rather than *your* values.

Limit the number of errors that you point out, and have a system in place for follow-through. If you feel compelled to note every single misplaced modifier, stray comma, and ill-chosen word, the students are unlikely to change anything in the future. Your red mark on the paper does not equal the student's learning, however dutiful those markings make you feel. I'd say this: if you don't have a way of having the student follow through on an error, don't point it out. Your follow-through can be in the form of a prescriptive lesson, such as an RxWrite system (see Chapter 7) or whole-class lessons that address a common problem that comes to light when you read a class set.

Shift your focus from error-based reading to strength-based reading of student papers. Rather than showing students examples of sentences that are burdened by errors, show them exemplary sentences. Exemplary sentences are more than just error-free: they are efficient, concise, vivid, clear, and strong, despite being complex. They get to be this way because of verb choice, absence of clutter, and use of punctuation that guides meaning. Many errors can be obviated when students learn how to *build* sentences rather than just fix up a mess.

Have students categorize their errors, and then key those error types to an accessible handbook. The handbook can be an online resource or a grammar book. But each student needs to know which parts of that grammar book get the heaviest use for their particular writing problems. Students can develop awareness of the kinds of errors that they are making repeatedly by keeping an error notebook. Have students reflect in their writing journal upon their own development as writers, including the kinds of errors that they struggle with and how concern about making those errors has affected their writing choices.

Don't do all of the work for students. If you find an error that you know has been taught repeatedly over the years (*there/their*, for example), simply put a check in the margin of the line in which the error appears and have the student locate and correct the error. I've found that it takes only a few minutes to re-check such corrections, and I do it as part of class; I don't collect all of the papers again, as doing so would be overwhelming. Most of the time, the kinds of errors that I would check in this way are ones that arise from carelessness, not ones that actually need instruction.

Summary

Errors give us important diagnostic information about what beginning writers understand about the code of academic writing. Errors are often a sign of growth in a writer. The writer may be trying out a new form of expression, creating sentences that are longer and more complex than he or she quite knows how to handle, or experimenting with a new kind of voice. This new kind of voice could be the academic voice that the young writer is trying to imitate. Or it could be that the young writer is trying to introduce some informal, conversational characteristics, like professionals do. Looked at this way, errors begin to lose their power to vex us and instead offer us diagnostic information about our students' quest to master a sophisticated writing style.

Appendix A

Rules for Clear and Accurate Writing

Over the course of my years as an English teacher, I compiled the best rules that I could find for guiding my students toward clear and accurate writing. That collection of rules follows. Included with each rule is a brief comment about how the observance of that rule *affects the reader*. Without consideration of how observance of a rule affects the reader, writers may mistakenly believe that rules are arbitrary. Writers need to think about readers, just as cooks need to think about diners. These rules give writers the perspective of readers.

Writing Rules

1. **The Rule of Diction:** Use the right word for the context and audience. *This will allow your reader to take you seriously.*

2. **The Rule of Joining Independent Clauses:** Don't send a boy to do a man's job! A comma alone is not sufficient to join two independent clauses. To join independent clauses, we need a semicolon or a comma along with a conjunction (*and, but, so*). *This will allow your reader to understand where your ideas begin and end and will eliminate confusion.*

3. **The Rule of Closeness:** Place all grammatical structures next to what they modify. *This will allow your reader to understand how your words relate to each other and will eliminate confusion.*

4. **The Rule of Positives:** Most messages are clearer when delivered in positive, rather than negative, form. *Your reader will appreciate this because your message will be readily accessible.*

5. **The Rule of Complete Sentences:** To test whether a group of words makes up a complete sentence, try placing "It is true that…" in front of the words. If you can do so, then you have a complete sentence. If not, then you don't. (Note: This rule will not work if the sentence begins with *and*, *but*, or *so*; however, such sentences can be complete

sentences anyway.) *For most academic circumstances, your reader is expecting complete sentences.*

6. **The Rule of Apostrophes:** Use apostrophes to indicate possessives and contractions. There is no apostrophe in the word *its* when it is used as a possessive pronoun. (*It's* always means *it is*.) *Your reader will appreciate your attention to detail.*

7. **The Rule of Hyphenation:** Hyphenate compound adjectives, that is, hyphenate adjectives that are formed out of two words, such as *man-eating* tiger. *Observing this rule will eliminate confusion.*

8. **The Rule of Conciseness:** Express yourself clearly in as few words as possible. Omit unnecessary words. *Your reader will appreciate your consideration.*

9. **The Rules of Agreement:**

    a. **Subject/verb:** The subject must agree with the verb. Objects of prepositions are not subjects, and should be ignored in subject/verb agreement. Hence, "A group of women is [a group is] enjoying the concert," rather than, "A group of women are enjoying the concert."

    b. **Pronoun/antecedent:** All pronouns refer to something that comes before them in the same sentence or a previous sentence. The word that the pronoun refers to is called the antecedent. The pronoun must agree with its antecedent. Because English has no generic singular pronoun, we run into a problem in sentences such as, "Everybody is to bring _____ own lunch." What to do? Modern stylists advise you to revise to avoid this dilemma. Hence, revise the sentence to, "All campers are to bring their own lunch," and the problem is solved! *If you observe the rules of agreement, your reader will not have to trip over mistakes.*

10. **The Rule of Pronoun Case:** Use the correct case of pronoun (subjective or objective). We don't usually run into problems when we have only one pronoun in a structure: "*I* saw a great movie. Ask *me* about it." But we sometimes run into problems when we add another person: "*Judi and I* saw a great movie. If you have any questions, ask *her or me*." Remember: the object of any preposition should be in the objective case. *Your reader will appreciate your attention to detail.*

11. **The Rules of Commas:** Remember LIES.

    a. **L: Lists.** The comma before the final item in a series is optional, but a bit more formal.

    b. **I: Introductions.** Place a comma before elements that precede the subject.

c. **E: Extra information.** Divide extra (nonessential) information of all kinds with a comma on each side of the extra information.

d. **S: Side-by-side sentences.** Divide independent clauses (sentences) with a comma and a conjunction.

(Note: Also observe the comma rules that apply to quotations.) *Your reader will appreciate observance of comma rules, because commas prevent word collision that results in confusion. Unnecessary commas impede comprehension.*

12. **The Rule of Active Voice:** In most cases, readers prefer the active voice to the passive voice. Use passive only when you wish to be evasive or diplomatic. For example:

Active voice: "She shoots. She scores."

Passive voice: Shooting is done by her. Scoring is done by her.

Your reader will appreciate the liveliness of your writing if you use active voice.

Appendix B

Spelling Instruction: A Guide for Teachers

- ◆ Understand how people learn to spell:
  - Most people learn to spell through a combination of explicit instruction (phonics, patterns, and rules) and receiving the visual cues of words as they read. Reading fosters correct spelling.
  - Everyone has personal spelling problems. Some people confuse certain words with others; some have trouble with certain kinds of letter combinations, word patterns, or applying rules and their exceptions. When we understand *why* we are misspelling a word, we can often fix the problem.
  - Therefore, it's important for us to help our students understand why they are misspelling certain words (where their confusion lies) as well as how they can fix the problem by applying their preferred learning styles.
- ◆ Traditional classroom practices that do *not* tend to promote better spelling:
  - Spelling tests. We find to our chagrin that students spell words correctly on a test, but then misspell the same words in context.
  - Demanding "look-ups." Yes, you can learn to spell a word once by looking it up in the dictionary. But as with spelling tests, the student is likely to misspell that same word in short order.
- ◆ Traditional classroom practices that *do* tend to promote better spelling:
  - Incorporating spelling instruction as you introduce subject-area terminology. As you're writing a word on the board, take a few seconds to emphasize how that word is spelled. (Added benefit: doing so will reinforce the meaning of the word.)

- As you help students learn new words, point out patterns. Words, especially Latinate words, tend to come in clusters. While teaching the word *median*, for example, you might want to point out its relationship to *mediate, mediation, remedial,* and *immediate.* Think etymologically. Sound-alike words almost always have a common root meaning somewhere in their history. (Added benefit: word associations foster durable learning.)

- Model the importance of spelling, especially of subject-area terminology. We don't "own" a word unless we can spell it. (Added benefit: students will tend to use words more readily if they are sure of the spelling.)

- Display subject-area words in your classroom. The visual cues will imprint the proper spelling. Even better, have students make word displays. (Added benefit: your room will look pretty.)

- Expect correct spelling. If you are uneasy taking points off for misspelled words, try adding bonus point for 100 percent correct spelling (but *not* at the expense of elevated vocabulary). (Added benefit: your gradebook will look pretty.

♦ Schoolwide practices that promote better spelling:

  - A universally accepted expectation that spelling will be an essential instructional component in all subject areas.

  - Posting key words and spelling rules in every classroom.

  - Facilitating the instructional practices described herein.

♦ Nontraditional, differentiated instruction practices that tend to promote better spelling:

  - To differentiate instruction in spelling, you might want to suggest that students choose one or more of the following strategies to conquer their spelling demons:

  1. *Visual reinforcement.* The more we see words that are spelled correctly, the better. *Never* deliberately show a misspelled word. Use color coding or exaggeration to point up the tricky part of the word. Do everything you can to create a visual imprint. Some people need to close their eyes and visualize a word.

  2. *Rhythm and auditory reinforcement.* Spell words aloud when introducing them. Try to find rhythmic patterns, such as *nec-ess-ary.* Rhythm is an extremely powerful memory cue.

Don't forget pronunciation. Many words get misspelled because they are mispronounced.

3. *Kinesthetic reinforcement.* This can come in the form of writing a word multiple times, especially if the writing is accompanied by visual and auditory cues. Air-writing works well for some people, as does tracing, writing the words across large surfaces, or writing them with tactile enhancements such as finger paint or shaving cream.

4. *Interpersonal reinforcement.* When students ask you how a word is spelled, take advantage of the teachable moment to explain everything you can about the word and its etymology. Teach words in clusters.

5. *Metacognitive reinforcement.* Have students keep a word journal and find patterns in the words that they tend to misspell. Encourage students to intellectualize about why they misspelled the word: Were they confusing it with another word? Unaware of a rule? Misapplying a rule? Mispronouncing the word?

6. *Whole word contour exercise.* Give students cardstock paper and have them write the words in letters large enough to cover the paper. Then, have them cut out the contour of the whole word with scissors. This is a good exercise because it provides a visual and a tactile model. Post the words.

7. *Patterns, associations, and rules.* Again, never learn or teach just one word at a time. Link the given word to others. Learning is strengthened through associations.

8. *Mnemonics.* These are tricks that help us remember. Some of these are rhythm-based, image-based, or slogans ("never be*lie*ve a *lie*"; "strawberry *s*hortcake de*ss*ert"; etc.).

9. *Words-within-words.* Point out *a rat* in *separate; iron* in *environment*, and so on.

10. *Connections between English spelling and Spanish, French, and Italian.* Show how Latinate words have spelling links.

11. *Syllabication.* Breaking words down into syllables allows students to learn words in accessible pieces and promotes learning about prefixes, roots, and suffixes.

12. *Communication.* Your students may have strategies to share that you don't know about. Open the floor.

13. *Modeling your own learning.* When you misspell a word, model for the students that you care about spelling the word correctly,

even though it is no big deal for a teacher to misspell a word. Show them how you intend to go about learning that word. Even better, ask students to help you think of a way to remember it.

14. *Internalization of the rules.* Some students will learn the rules by memorizing; others, by translating them into a flow chart or other kind of graphic.

15. *Development of a repertoire.* Encourage, promote, and model the development of a repertoire of the above strategies.

Useful Spelling Rules

1. **The Prefix Rule:** Adding a prefix is the easiest kind of change you can make to a word. The base word does not change when a prefix is added. Sometimes, the last letter of the prefix is the same as the first letter of the base word: *misspell, disservice, unnecessary, irregular, dissatisfied.* Usually, however, prefixed words have single letters where the prefix meets the base word: *disappear, disapprove, unattractive, insincere, mismatched.*

2. **The I Before E Rule:** It's *I* before *e* except after *c*, or when sounded as *a*, as in *neighbor* or *sleigh*. Hence, *fiery, believe, relieve, friend;* and *receive, conceive, perceive, foreign, reign, weight, freight.*

3. **The Suffix Rules:**

   a. Does the word have one syllable? Does the word end in one vowel, one consonant? Does the suffix begin with a vowel? Then double the consonant: *run, running.*

   b. Does the word have two or more syllables? Does the word end with a consonant-vowel-consonant pattern? Does the suffix begin with a vowel? Does the accent fall on the syllable just before the suffix? Then double the consonant: *admit, admitted; commit, committing.*

   c. Does the word end in silent *e?* Does the suffix begin with a vowel? Then drop the *e: hope, hoping; give, giving.*

   d. Is *y* the last letter of the word? Does the suffix begin with a consonant? Then change *y* to *I* before adding the suffix: *carry, carried; bury, burial.*

   e. Is the suffix *-ly, -ness,* or *-ment?* Then do not change the spelling of the base word **unless** it ends in *y: careful, carefully; fond, fondness; merry, merriment.*

f. The *-ible, -able* rule:

If the root is not a complete word, add *-ible: visible, edible, eligible, legible.*

If the root is a complete word, add *-able: suitable, dependable, reliable.*

Drop the silent *e* to add *-able: likable, valuable, advisable.*

g. The *-ion* rule:

If the root ends in *-ct,* add *-ion: select, selection.*

If the root ends in *-ss,* add *-ion: discuss, discussion.*

If the root ends in *-te,* drop the *e* and add *-ion: educate, education.*

If the root ends in *-it,* change the *t* to *s* and add *-sion: permit, permission.*

If the root ends in a vowel followed by *-de,* drop the *e,* change the *d* to *s* and add *-sion: explode, explosion.*

Source: Sipe, R. B. (2003). *They Still Can't Spell? Understanding and Supporting Challenged Spellers in Middle and High School.* Portsmouth, NH: Heinemann.

References

Benjamin, A. (2005). *Writing in the content areas* (2nd ed.). Larchmont, NY: Eye on Education.

Bizzell, P. (1982). Cognition, context, and certainty: What we need to know about writing. *PRE/TEXT, 3*(3), 213–243.

Fuller, Renee. In Context: *A quarterly of humane sustainable culture.* http://www.context.org/ICLIB/IC27/Fuller.htm. "The Primacy of Story." 1991. p. 26.

Gere, A. R., Christenbury, L., & Sassi, K. (2005). *Writing on demand: Best practices and strategies for success.* Portsmouth, NH: Heinemann.

Gocsik, K. (n.d.). *Teaching modes of discourse.* Retrieved March 15, 2006, from http://www.dartmouth.edu/~writing/materials/faculty/pedagogies/modes.shtml

Kinneavy, James. Graduate Research. The basic aims of discourse. http://danitasresearch.blogspot.com/2004/10/basic-aims-of-discourse-by-james.htmlober. Retrieved Oct 17, 2004.

Learn great ideas, but teach to the test. (2005, July 13). *The New York Times*, p. 8, section B.

National Commission on Writing in America's Schools and Colleges. (2003). *The Neglected R: The Need for a Writing Revolution*, p. 6.

National Council of Teachers of English. (1974, Reaffirmed, 2003). *Students right to their own language.* Urbana, Illinois.

National Council of Teachers of English. Good writing instruction, not testing, is the best preparation for college. http://www.ncte.org/about/over/inbox/news/120541.htm?source=gs. Urbana, Illinois. Retrieved May 3, 2005.

National Writing Project & Nagin, C. (2003). *Because writing matters.* San Francisco: Jossey-Bass.

Noguchi, R. (1991). *Grammar and the teaching of writing: Limits and possibilities.* Urbana, IL: National Council of Teachers of English.

Pike-Baky, M., & Fleming, G. (2005). *Prompted to write: Building on-demand writing skills, grades 6–12.* San Francisco: Jossey-Bass.

Scheir, W., & Touchette, A. (2004). *Roadmap to the New Jersey HSPA Language Arts Literacy.* New York: Random House.

Schuster, E. H. (2003). *Breaking the rules: Liberating writers through innovative grammar instruction.* Portsmouth, NH: Heinemann.

Shaughnessy, M. (1977). *Errors and expectations: A guide for the teacher of basic writing.* New York: Oxford University Press.

Sipe, R. B. (2003). *They still can't spell? Understanding and supporting challenged spellers in middle and high school* Portsmouth, NH: Heinemann.

Spandell, V., & Stiggins, R. (1990). *Creating writers: Linking assessment and writing instruction.* New York: Longman.

Touchstones Discussion Project. (1986). *Touchstones: Volume A.* CMZ Publishers.

Vanderveen, P. (2005). *Acing the state writing assessment: A handbook of exercises.* Cheswold, DE: Prestwick House.

Zwier, L. J. (2002). *Building academic vocabulary.* Ann Arbor: University of Michigan.